Best Hikes Near
SAN DIEGO

HELP US KEEP THIS GUIDE UP TO DATE

Every effort has been made by the authors and editors to make this guide as accurate and useful as possible. However, many things can change after a guide is published—trails are rerouted, regulations change, techniques evolve, facilities come under new management, and so on.

We would appreciate hearing from you concerning your experiences with this guide and how you feel it could be improved and kept up to date. While we may not be able to respond to all comments and suggestions, we'll take them to heart, and we'll also make certain to share them with the authors. Please send your comments and suggestions to the following address:

GPP
Reader Response/Editorial Department
P.O. Box 480
Guilford, CT 06437

Or you may e-mail us at: editorial@globepequot.com

Thanks for your input, and happy trails!

Best Hikes Near
SAN DIEGO

ALEXANDER SAKARU GOYA AND LYNN GOYA

FALCONGUIDES

GUILFORD, CONNECTICUT
HELENA, MONTANA

AN IMPRINT OF GLOBE PEQUOT PRESS

To buy books in quantity for corporate use
or incentives, call **(800) 962–0973**
or e-mail **premiums@GlobePequot.com.**

FALCONGUIDES®

FalconGuides is an imprint of Globe Pequot Press.
Falcon, FalconGuides, and Outfit Your Mind are registered trademarks of Morris Book Publishing, LLC.

Interior photos by Alexander Sakaru Goya

Text design: Sheryl P. Kober
Layout: Maggie Peterson
Project editor: Gregory Hyman

Maps by Hartdale Maps © Morris Book Publishing, LLC

TOPO! Explorer software and SuperQuad source maps courtesy of National Geographic Maps. For information about TOPO! Explorer, TOPO!, and Nat Geo Maps products, go to www.topo.com or www.natgeomaps.com.

Library of Congress Cataloging-in-Publication Data is available on file.

ISBN 978-0-7627-6393-1

Printed in the United States of America

10 9 8 7 6 5 4 3 2 1

Contents

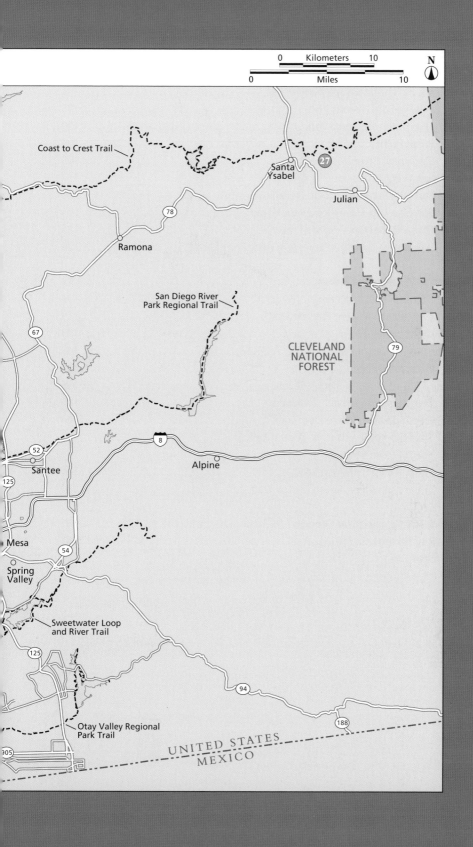

Acknowledgments

Nothing is done in a vacuum, and that is especially true for this book.

Thank you to Nicholas Martinez and the San Diego Tourism Department for your help. Thank you to the California Coastal Trails team for the use of their maps as part of our base maps. What a great project!

Laura Senn is a favorite hiking partner, even when she isn't there! Thanks for the hiking tips, however, and all your other help. Thank you to our editor, John Burbidge, for his patience and guidance. Thank you Sari and Jim Hotchkiss for the best coffee in town and the chats that went with it. To our family: Chloe, who let us borrow her fancy new car. Driving around without AC would not have been nearly as pleasant. Besides, a clutch added to the fun. Also to Alan, for helping with all the little things it took to make this project work and for just putting up with us in general. And Seiji, you get great coffee and are a wonderful hiking companion. Now that you can drive, we're going to raise our expectations of your participation for the next book.

Grandma Berchenbriter, thank you for inspiring our career as hiking guide coauthors. We would never have done it without you! We did miss the great meals you always had waiting for us on our return. Refrigerator leftovers somehow didn't compare.

Grandma Goya, we're working on getting a guide for your hometown. Can we stay with you?

There are always those in any effort who extend a hand when it could just as easily be left at their side. For this guide that would be Bob and Deborah Young. They gave us a gorgeous place to stay in the heart of downtown San Diego (wish we had had time to take better advantage of it!), and they shared their extensive history of hiking the county. But most important, we were grateful for the friendly faces that welcomed us in, even when we arrived in the middle of the night. Thanks for sharing a beer, a story, and more than a few meals. We don't know what we would have done without you.

Stunning views such as this make Cowles Mountain a must-visit for San Diego–area hikers. See Hike 14.

Introduction

With its proximity to the ocean, varying microclimates, and easy access to trails, San Diego is one of the best metropolitan areas in the world to go hiking. Forty-one county parks, sixteen state parks, and a variety of city parks wind in and around San Diego, and all are accessible year-round. In this area there are no excessively scorching hot days, no deep snowdrifts, and few prohibitively rainy days. San Diego temperatures rarely exceed 90 degrees Fahrenheit (average of four days out of the year), making it pleasant to be outside in every season. In general, most hikes are well marked, well maintained, and well traveled. The barriers to hiking are so low in San Diego that there are few reasons not to participate. It is difficult, however, to find solitude even on the most remote hikes within the county. People are outdoors everywhere, biking, walking their dogs, pushing strollers, running, in-line skating, and in general enjoying the fine San Diego weather.

Fortunately for San Diegans, the state, county, and local governments continue to build new recreational access points and protect existing environments. Even as this book goes to print, a large-scale project is under way to restore much of the wetlands in the San Dieguito coastal area. San Dieguito was once the largest lagoon in the region and still has the largest watershed. These efforts will both restore many aquatic functions of the lagoon and provide habitat for endangered wildlife. An added bonus will be miles of new trails, which will allow hikers to observe and enjoy the area as it regenerates.

New trails and access points are constantly being built. The County Trails Program has 1,300 miles of proposed trails on its master plan, including 650 miles of multiuse trails. The county is connecting and extending trails to create nine regional trails that will take hikers from south to north and from its coasts to its deserts. Keep abreast of the developments as the following trails are enhanced, connected, and expanded: the California Coastal Trail, the California Riding and Hiking Trail, the Coast to Crest Trail, the Juan Bautista de Anza Historic Trail, the Otay Valley Regional Park Trail, the Pacific Crest National Scenic Trail, the San Diego River Park Regional Trail, the Sweetwater Loop and River Trail, and the Trans-County Trail. We've included sections of most of these trails throughout this guide. Download a copy of the complete trail proposal at www.sdparks.org. We've also included city and state trails.

Plans for new trails don't mean that existing trails aren't plentiful. The individual parks and recreation areas in San Diego County would be considered small by Western standards, yet they more than make up for it in variety and availability. Parks in the middle of dense urban areas can feel remote and natural, while areas farther inland can be extremely popular even in the middle of the week. And while we all have our favorite hikes, there really is no bad spot to hike in San Diego—one finds a great view, a feeling of isolation, or a spirit of friendly camaraderie.

At Sunset Cliffs hikers can find their own private spot to watch the sun sink into the sea. See Hike 9.

Along the way you will see many trademarks of San Diego. Navy, Marine, and Coast Guard bases and training grounds have a long history in this city. The city is also known as "the birthplace of naval aviation" and is one of the chief bases for the U.S. Pacific Fleet. Many of our hikes take you to places where you can see the fleet or skim the line next to working bases or training facilities. You'll be able to see magnificent war ships, ancient sailing ships, and fleets of yachts and sailboats during many of our hikes. These hikes offer people who love watercraft a wealth of options to observe boats of all shapes, sizes, and functions up close and personal.

Of course San Diego is known for nothing if not its beaches. While the wide, sunny beaches are enough to draw crowds, you'll find that the density falls off rather rapidly as you move away from the parking areas. Often a short hop in the right direction is all it takes to find a quieter spot. Beaches around Carlsbad, Encinitas, and Imperial Beach are especially good locations to get away from the crowds. In fact, don't be surprised if you find yourself alone on an isolated beach with nothing but birds and dolphins as companions. We've included some of our favorite beach hikes, letting you know how to find the beach access points and what to expect when you get there. Note that some areas are impassable during high tide as the ocean rises against the cliffs; be sure to check our guidelines before setting out.

The San Diego area is so much more than just the sum of its parts. From forests to lagoons, urban condo dwellers to beach nuts, the unique character of the area and the populace permeates through. On most every hike you'll find residents who are curious, friendly, and generally in a good mood. We had a great time working on this guide. We hope you enjoy this unique, very special place.

Weather

San Diego's climate is sometimes referred to as "arid Mediterranean," a combination of a Mediterranean climate to the north and the more semi-arid to the south and east. Thus San Diego has generally warm, sunny summers and mild winters, with most rainfall occurring between November and March. Due to the area's varying topography, the climate can change rather abruptly over a relatively short distance, although the weather is almost always more temperate right along the coast. Inland, the temperatures can rise quickly, so bring your best sun gear. On the coast you might need a jacket in midday in mid-July. Wear layers, expect the sun—eventually—and bring plenty of water and sunscreen. If you are lucky enough to get caught in a sudden rainstorm, just lift your face to the sky and enjoy.

Waterfowl stalk in the shallow waters at Border Field. See Hike 29.

Critters

Much has changed since settlers first arrived in San Diego. Yet populations of mule deer and mountain lions still roam the county. Bighorn sheep can be found in the eastern areas, and diamondback rattlesnakes are fairly common on the dry, desertlike paths of East County. An exquisite variety of birds can be seen throughout the area. Many species of pelicans and terns are quite common near the deltas, and birds of prey such as hawks, falcons, and bald eagles can be seen inland. In addition, the county is a major flight path for migratory birds.

During winter, California gray whales can be seen along the coast as they migrate to and from their tropical calving lagoons. (San Diego harbor was once a calving location. Period reports say that the bay was so thick with whales that you could walk across it on their backs. Whalers soon put an end to that.) The past few years have seen occasional whale sightings in the harbor as well as a healthy return of migrating gray whales. Who knows? Maybe someday they'll again be thick enough in the bay that you can walk to Coronado on their backs.

Hazards

San Diego has so many microclimates that the list of native plants and animals is impressive. However, don't be fooled into eating those beautiful plants unless you have an excellent guide to edible plants. And while we adore most of the wildlife, there are a few to take note of while hiking. Be aware of these potential hazards.

Brambles and Cactus

If you run afoul of brambles and cacti along the trail, take a piece of duct tape, stick it over the afflicted area, and use it to pull thorns or spines out of the skin.

Ticks

The main problem with ticks, other than that they are ugly and suck your blood, is that they can carry Lyme disease, a serious, potentially life-altering illness. Deer ticks carrying Lyme disease have been found in San Diego County. If you find a tick on you, put it in a plastic bag and take it to the health department for testing.

Bugs

There are generally few flying insects around San Diego. However, mosquitoes are sometimes encountered. As a precaution, wear long pants and a long-sleeved shirt and have insect repellent on hand, especially in the northeast part of the county and anywhere with fresh water.

Hunters

San Diego's wilderness areas are being restored with the cooperation of hunters, anglers, and other sports enthusiasts, so share the trail and be aware of hunting seasons. If you are hiking during hunting season, wear some blaze-orange clothing so that you are not mistaken for a wild giraffe.

Rattlesnakes

There are thirty-three species of snakes in San Diego County. The diamondback rattlesnake is the only venomous one and can be identified by the diamond-shaped markings on its back and its triangular head. If bitten, seek medical attention immediately. Do not attempt to suck out the venom or apply ice to the wound. The best solution is to calmly walk back to your vehicle and get to a hospital as quickly as possible. If your cell phone has a signal, call 911. If you think you are an hour or more away from medical care, wrap the area between the bite and your heart to restrict (but not cut off) blood flow. (For instance, if bitten on the ankle, wrap your calf.) Snakebites are rarely lethal these days if medical treatment is obtained quickly.

Skunks, Opossums, and Raccoons

Avoid contact if you see a skunk, opossum, or raccoon during your travels. Each of these animals can carry rabies and can attack if they feel threatened. Under no circumstance should you feed wild animals or leave out food that can be easily accessed. Human contact can make these creatures aggressive and dangerous. If

Some San Diego–area trails bring hikers within close proximity to cliffs, which can be unstable. Please be aware of your surroundings.

you see a stuck, injured, or trapped animal, do not attempt to rescue it. Contact a ranger or park official instead. As with all wildlife, these animals should be viewed and appreciated from a distance.

Safety and Preparation

Hiking in San Diego County is generally safe. Still, hikers should take care:

- Let people know where you are going and when you expect to return. Wear a good whistle when hiking in the backcountry so that if you become lost or injured, you have a low-energy way to let people know where you are.

- Don't drink from San Diego's streams, rivers, creeks, or lakes.

- Carry a backpack with water, binoculars, a snack, and this guidebook. Pick up a bird, butterfly, and native plant book for good measure.

- Keep children under careful watch, especially around rivers, caves, cliffs, and steep hills. Don't let children out of your sight in mountain lion areas.

- Watch for falling rocks.

Leave No Trace

As San Diego works to restore our wonderful natural heritage, we should make sure that we do it right this time, adopting the Leave No Trace ideology of zero impact: Leave only footprints, take only pictures. Don't disturb wildlife. We, as trail users and advocates, must be especially vigilant to make sure our passage leaves no lasting mark.

San Diego County Boundaries and Corridors

For the purposes of this guide, all hikes are within San Diego County. Directions to the trailheads begin from one of the major highways running north–south or east–west. Hikes in this guide are located along I-5, I-8, I-15, CA 1, and CA 52.

Land Management

The following government and private organizations manage most of the public lands described in this guide and can provide additional information on the featured hikes and other trails in their service areas:

Bureau of Land Management, 1661 South Fourth St., El Centro, CA 92243; (760) 337-4400; www.blm.gov/ca/st/en/fo/elcentro/esdrmp.html
County of San Diego, County Operations Center, 5555 Overland Ave., Building #2, San Diego, CA 92123; (858) 694-2212; http://sdpublic.sdcounty.ca.gov/portal/page?_pageid=93,298331&_dad=portal&_schema=PORTAL

Port of San Diego, 3165 Pacific Hwy., San Diego, CA 92101-1128; (619) 686-6200; www.portofsandiego.org/recreation.html

San Diego Association of Governments (SANDAG), 401 B St., Suite 800, San Diego, CA 92101; (619) 699-1900; www.sandag.org

City of San Diego Park and Recreation, 202 C St., MS 37C, San Diego, CA 92101; (619) 236-6643; www.sandiego.gov/park-and-recreation/

City of Encinitas, 505 South Vulcan Ave., Encinitas, CA 92024; (760) 633-2740; http://www.ci.encinitas.ca.us/Contact+Us.htm

California State Parks, San Diego Coast District, 4477 Pacific Hwy., San Diego, CA 92110-3136; (619) 688-3260; www.parks.ca.gov/parkindex/region_info .asp?id=10&tab=1

California Department of Fish and Game, DFG Lands Program, 1812 Ninth St., Sacramento, CA 95811; www.dfg.ca.gov/lands/er/region5/

Handcarved steps at Los Peñasquitos Canyon Preserve invite hikers to ascend. See Hike 19.

How to Use This Guide

This guide is designed to be simple and easy to use. Each hike is described with a map and summary information that delivers the trail's vital statistics including length, difficulty, fees and permits, park hours, canine compatibility, and trail contacts. Directions to the trailhead are also provided, along with a general description of what you'll see along the way. A detailed route finder (Miles and Directions) estimates mileages between significant landmarks along the trail.

Difficulty Ratings

For experienced hikers, these are all easy hikes. But since easy is a relative term, we have ranked the hikes as easy, moderate, or more challenging in the hike specs.

Easy hikes are generally short and flat, taking no longer than a few hours to complete and many taking an hour or less. Most of the beach hikes fit into this category.

Moderate hikes involve increased distance and relatively mild changes in elevation; most take one to two hours to complete. If you are unable to do the entire hike, there are often secondary access points that will let you enjoy the hike while still remaining in your comfort zone.

More challenging hikes feature some steep stretches, uneven surfaces, greater distances, and rock scrambling or require more than two hours to complete. They take more gumption but can often be modified for those with limited abilities. If you can make the entire hike, the payoff is worth it.

Approximate hiking times are based on the assumption that on flat ground, most walkers average 2 miles per hour. Adjust that rate by your level of fitness and you have a ballpark hiking duration. Be sure to add more time if you plan to picnic or take part in other activities like birding or photography. Many of these hikes are so gorgeous that you should add time just for gawking at the scenery.

Hike Selection

San Diego is consistently ranked one of the fittest cities in the country, and outdoor recreation has always been especially important to San Diegans. Even with more than five million people living in the greater San Diego metropolitan area, quality trails exist within fifteen minutes of almost anywhere in the county. San Diego is blessed with magnificent beaches, so we've selected hikes at or around our favorite beaches. Most people forget that beaches make wonderful hiking destinations, with the constantly varying light and the better than average chance to spot wildlife on shore or slightly out to sea. We've done our best to help you experience the magnificent shore with your clothes on.

In general we've tried to cover new trails that may not appear in other guide-books. City and county governments, nonprofit agencies, and state agencies are all actively trying to expand and interconnect existing trail systems to meet the rising demand for outdoor recreational opportunities from San Diego's residents and visitors. We have done our best to provide an accurate, up-to-date guide with a wide appeal. Some hikes are short, easy strolls; others are more strenuous and can take an entire afternoon. In the course of your travels, we hope we can introduce you to new places and trails not directly covered in the pages of this book. San Diego County offers much more than could ever be covered in one book. Once you get started, you'll find more gems than you could ever imagine. We hope you enjoy the constantly evolving adventure. We do. See you on the trails!

On the Guy Fleming Trail, scenic seating areas allow hikers welcome respite. See Hike 16.

Trail Finder

Hike No.	Hike Name	Best Beach Hikes	Best Hikes with a View	Best Hikes for Whale Watching	Best Hikes with Kids	Best Birding Hikes	Best Historical Hikes	Best Hikes with Your Dog
1	Balboa Park				•		•	
2	Batiquitos Lagoon				•	•		
3	Belmont Park Beach	•			•			
4	Coronado Ferry		•		•			
5	Hotel Del Coronado Beach Walk							
6	Point Loma Tide Pools				•			
7	San Diego Port							
8	Shelter Island				•			
9	Sunset Cliffs			•				•
10	Sweetwater Regional Park							•
11	Black's Beach	•						
12	Blue Sky Ecological Reserve							
13	Broken Hill Trail							
14	Cowles Mountain		•					
15	Dog Beach Mudflat				•	•		•
16	Guy Fleming Trail		•					
17	Ocean Beach Pier							
18	Beacon's Beach to Moonlight Beach	•						
19	Los Peñasquitos Canyon Preserve						•	
20	Old Presidio Historic Hike		•				•	

Trail Finder

Hike No.	Hike Name	Best Beach Hikes	Best Hikes with a View	Best Hikes for Whale Watching	Best Hikes with Kids	Best Birding Hikes	Best Historical Hikes	Best Hikes with Your Dog
21	Otay Valley Regional Park							
22	Razor Point							
23	San Diego River Reserve							
24	San Dieguito County Park				●			●
25	San Elijo Lagoon—La Orilla Trail							●
26	San Elijo Lagoon—Rios Avenue Trail							
27	Santa Ysabel Open Space Preserve							
28	Wilderness Gardens Preserve					●		
29	Border Field State Park							
30	Cabrillo Monument Bayside Trail			●			●	
31	Carlsbad Beach							
32	Imperial Beach Pier			●				
33	Kwaay Paay Peak						●	
34	La Jolla Shores to Black's Beach	●						
35	Manchester Reserve							●
36	Presidio Park—White Deer Trail				●			
37	San Elijo Reserve Nature Center					●		
38	Silver Strand Stretch							
39	Tijuana Estuary—North McCoy Trail							
40	Tijuana Estuary—South McCoy Trail							

Map Legend

Transportation

≡⑤≡ Freeway/Interstate Highway

≡⑩①≡ U.S. Highway

≡⑧≡ State Highway

==== Unpaved Road

├──┼──┤ Railroad

Trails

▪▪▪▪▪▪ Selected Route

▪ ▪ ▪ ▪ ▪ Trail or Fire Road

⟶ Direction of Travel

Water Features

Body of Water

River or Creek

Wetland or Meadow

Waterfalls

Land Features

Local & State Parks

National Forest &
Wilderness Areas

Sand Area

Tidal Flat

Symbols

⋈ Bridge

▪ Building/Point of Interest

▲ Campground

⚑ Gate

❓ Information Center

☖ Lighthouse

▲ Mountain/Peak

🅿 Parking

⊞ Picnic Area

📋 Ranger Station

🚻 Restroom

❀ Scenic View

○ Towns and Cities

⑳ Trailhead

Popular, Heavily Trafficked Hikes

The same erosion mechanics that make tide pools possible can also create these dramatic, sweeping cliffs. See Hike 6.

Most hiking guides are organized by location, but as a twenty-year resident of San Diego, I know that San Diegans don't typically think that way. We know the hikes near our house and near our best friend's condo, because we do those all the time. We all have our secret, favorite hiking locations that we share with special friends, and we have our even more secret spots that we don't.

We've divided the hikes in this guide based on the hiking experience you are after. Some are popular and always crowded—but that's okay because San Diego is America's Party Town. Some are readily accessible but give you an opportunity to think you might be alone, and some are truly islands of isolation in paradise.

In this first section we invite you to invite your friends. Sometimes it seems as though all of San Diego's three million residents are out hiking with you. Some days, that's okay. It is the people watching as well as the planet watching that draws you out. Sharing the experience is part of the experience.

The hikes in this section are hikes to share with buddies and even buddies' buddies—even if you haven't met them yet. We have almost universally found that fellow hikers are friendly and respond to a quick smile and "hi." We've made long-term friends through these kinds of chance encounters. Except they aren't really by chance. Because if you are out there on a popular peak with your legs still burning from the climb and you turn to the person nearby and say, "Wow, what a view!" you know you already have something in common. Hikers—even in these popular destinations—have a way of soaking in the beauty and enjoying their own inner peace as long as everybody respects one another's space.

These hikes are popular because they are easily accessible, offer great views, and for the most part can be modified to accommodate any level of fitness. If you haven't hiked these hikes, you really haven't experienced San Diego. Look for us on the trails—and don't forget to smile as we cross paths.

The Crystal Pier, as seen from Belmont Park, is one of the iconic places to stay in San Diego. See Hike 3.

Balboa Park

Established in 1868, Balboa Park is one of the oldest dedicated recreation areas in the country. The park is home to fifteen major museums and a variety of themed gardens, performance venues, and the world-renowned San Diego Zoo. Its 1,200 acres and the diverse mix of horticulture, art, and culture are why Balboa Park has been named one of the Best Parks in the World by the Project for Public Places.

Start: Park entrance at the corner of Upas Street and Sixth Avenue
Distance: 2.8 miles out and back
Approximate hiking time: 2 hours
Difficulty: Easy
Trail surface: Paved trail and sidewalk, some dirt paths
Best season: Year-round
Other trail users: Couples, children, old men on their way to play boccie ball
Canine compatibility: Leashed dogs allowed
Fees and permits: No fees or permits required
Schedule: Open 24 hours a day; visitor center is open 9:30 a.m. to 4:30 p.m. daily, and museum hours vary by institution
Maps: USGS Point Loma; park map available online at www.balboapark.org/maps/TrailMap-6th-Upas.pdf
Trail contacts: Balboa Park, 1549 El Prado, Balboa Park, San Diego, CA 92101; (619) 239-0512
Special considerations: Public transportation map available at http://www.balboapark.org/maps/directions.php
Other: Museum admissions are free to residents on a rotating basis on Tuesdays throughout the month.

Finding the trailhead:
From CA 163 south, exit onto University Avenue, heading toward downtown. Continue straight, merging into Sixth Avenue. Begin the trail at the corner of Upas Street and Sixth Avenue. The trailhead begins on Balboa Drive at the large wooden map of the park. GPS: N32.740938 / W117.159491

THE HIKE

Built as City Park in 1868 to overlook New Town (present-day downtown San Diego), Balboa Park is one of the most beloved places in all San Diego. The park has been an important part of the town almost since day one. Only two years after the park was established, a law was passed declaring that "[Balboa Park is] to be held in trust forever by the municipal authorities of said city for the purpose of a park." When a bill was quietly introduced in 1870 to break up the park and sell parts for commercial purposes, residents rose up and petitioned Sacramento until the bill was killed in the legislature.

Today Balboa Park is the cultural, artistic, and recreational heart of the city. The resident Old Globe Theater produces fifteen plays and musicals every year, and one of the oldest youth theater programs in the United States is located within the park. Free performances on the world's largest pipe organ are held every Sunday at 2:00 p.m. throughout the year and Monday evening at 7:30 p.m. during summer. If you're looking for exercise, Morley Field Sports Complex includes a golf course, baseball fields, tennis courts, archery ranges, a swimming pool, a disc golf course, and playgrounds.

Along the path described here you will pass through two of the park's famous gardens: the Trees for Health Garden and the Botanical Building. The Trees for Health Garden was planted in 1995 to educate parkgoers on medicinal plants. Birds love the trees too. The Botanical Building is one of the largest lath structures

The reflection pond is one of the most popular stops in Balboa Park.

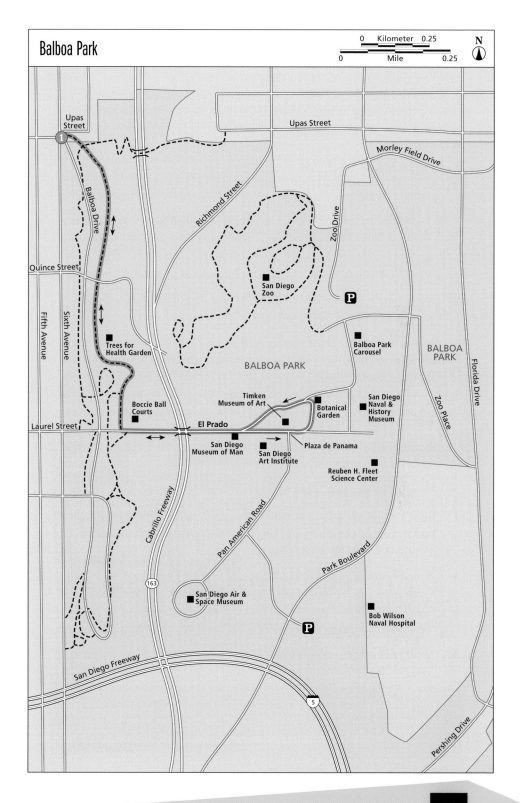

Balboa Park

Upas Street

Upas Street

Morley Field Drive

Richmond Street

Zoo Drive

Balboa Drive

Quince Street

San Diego Zoo

BALBOA PARK

P

Fifth Avenue

Sixth Avenue

Trees for Health Garden

Balboa Park Carousel

BALBOA PARK

Florida Drive

Boccie Ball Courts

Timken Museum of Art

Botanical Garden

San Diego Naval & History Museum

Zoo Place

Laurel Street

El Prado

San Diego Museum of Man

San Diego Art Institute

Plaza de Panama

Cabrillo Freeway

Reuben H. Fleet Science Center

Pan American Road

Park Boulevard

163

San Diego Air & Space Museum

P

Bob Wilson Naval Hospital

San Diego Freeway

5

Pershing Drive

0   Kilometer   0.25

0   Mile   0.25

N

in the world and was built for the 1915–16 Panama-California Exposition. It houses more than 2,100 plant specimens including cycads, ferns, orchids, other tropical plants, and palms. Although always one of the most popular places in the park, it is particularly stunning when the flowers bloom in spring. The reflection pool in front of the garden is filled with koi and water lilies that make it a favorite spot for photographers.

If you have time, the Balboa Park Carousel is one of the few carousels left with hand-carved wooden animals. Kids and adults can still try to catch the brass ring as they whirl around, something only a handful of carousels in the world still offer. The park offers unstructured strolls with many lovely vistas, but it also has trails that take you throughout the park and offer surprising solitude.

MILES AND DIRECTIONS

0.0   Start from the park entrance at Sixth Avenue and Upas Street and proceed down the path to the left (northeast) of the road.

0.3   A Trees for Health Garden sign appears on your left. Observe the medicinal plants as you make your way through the garden. Cross Quince Street and continue along the path.

0.5   Enter what is often referred to as an "urban forest." Many of these trees were planted in the park's early days.

0.7   Proceed left as you reach the boccie ball courts. Head around them to reach El Prado and then head left across the bridge.

1.2   Arrive at the fountain. This area is called Plaza de Panama.

1.3   Enter the Botanical Building and observe the rare and exotic plants. The building entrance with its lily ponds is one of the most popular places for photographers in the park.

1.4   Proceed straight out of the building past the reflecting pool. Feel free to make a wish, but please don't throw anything in the water. Then hit El Prado again. Turn right and head back the way you came. (**Option:** Explore the wonderful museums Balboa Park has to offer.)

2.8   Arrive back at the park entrance.

Before venturing into the park, visit the Balboa Park Visitor Center to learn about the park's interesting history.

Batiquitos Lagoon

This 3.2-mile hike runs along the northern section of a 610-acre lagoon and ecological preserve located in Carlsbad, California. Birders can expect to find great blue herons and snowy egrets year-round, while many species of terns, pelicans, and other birds can be found during migratory seasons.

Start: The Gabbiano Lane cul-de-sac

Distance: 3.2 miles out and back

Approximate hiking time: 1.5 hours

Difficulty: Easy

Trail surface: Wide dirt paths

Best season: Year-round; spring and fall for migratory birds

Other trail users: Group walks, painters, summer kids' camp

Canine compatibility: Leashed dogs allowed

Fees and permits: No fees or permits required

Schedule: Park open sunrise to sunset; nature center open 9:00 a.m. to 12:30 p.m. Mon–Fri; 9:00 a.m. to 3:00 p.m. Sat and Sun

Maps: USGS Encinitas

Trail contacts: Batiquitos Lagoon Nature Center, 7380 Gabbiano Lane, Carlsbad, CA 92011; (760) 931-0800; www.batiquitos foundation.org

Batiquitos Lagoon Ecological Reserve, 7102 Batiquitos Dr., Carlsbad, CA 92009; (858) 467-4201

Special considerations: Bring binoculars for observing wildlife.

Other: Restroom, telephone, and water are available when the nature center is open.

Finding the trailhead: Take I-5 (San Diego Freeway) north past Encinitas. As you enter the city of Carlsbad, you will cross over Batiquitos Lagoon. Take an immediate right onto Poinsettia Lane. Shortly after, turn right onto Batiquitos Drive and make another right down Gabbiano Lane. Parking and trail access are available at the end of the street or on Piovana Court. GPS: N33.56244 / W117.180835

Batiquitos Lagoon

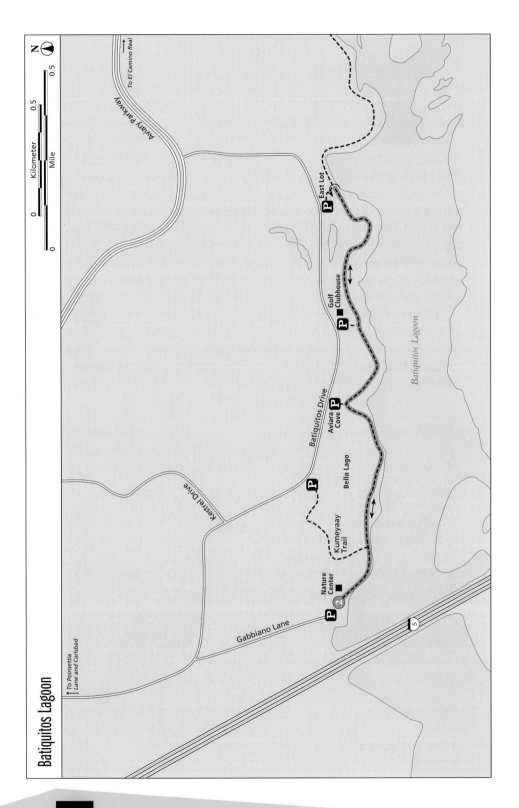

Popular, Heavily Trafficked Hikes

THE HIKE

Batiquitos Lagoon is one of the few remaining coastal wetlands in Southern California. Originally carved out by receding glaciers during the last ice age, the lagoon has been a haven for wildlife and early peoples as far back as 8,000 years ago. At that time the lagoon was much deeper, with heavy water exchange from the ocean. This began to change in the 1870s, when the surrounding area was opened up to homesteading by the U.S. government. The lagoon was affected by the gradual population increase, culminating in the construction of I-5, when the mouth of the lagoon was mostly closed to accommodate the bridge. This, along with agricultural runoff and the damming of fresh water into Batiquitos Lagoon, stopped the flow of water to the ocean, which had washed silt from the lagoon into the sea. Restoration projects have dredged the waterway to reopen its mouth, allowing the natural currents to once again ebb and flow between the ocean and the lagoon.

While the trailhead listed here is close to the nature center, access and parking are also available at four points along Batiquitos Drive. Batiquitos Lagoon Nature Center is run entirely by volunteers who, in addition to managing the reserve, host periodic nature walks throughout the year. Self-guided tour pamphlets are available at the center and are a great way to bone up on local plant and animal life.

The Batiquitos Lagoon path is wide and accessible, perfect for someone looking for a quick, convenient stroll.

(*Note:* An optional path to the right (west) takes you under the I-5 bridge. Fishing is permitted in this area but nowhere else in the lagoon.)

The sound of traffic from I-5 fades as you round the first corner, heading along the length of the lagoon to your left. The ocean breeze and tall shade trees make the hike pleasant and cool even during the height of summer. We observed runners, painters, and schoolchildren making use of the trail. Even during midday, waterfowl and hummingbirds are common sights. I was fortunate enough to watch a 6-foot rattlesnake cross the trail as I sat on one of the shaded benches placed strategically along the path. We both appeared to enjoy our noonday stroll.

MILES AND DIRECTIONS

0.0 Start at the trailhead on Gabbiano Lane, where a large sign discusses the lagoon and the Batiquitos Lagoon Foundation. Head left along the lagoon.

0.1 Arrive at the Batiquitos Lagoon Nature Center.

0.3 A tributary trail leads up the canyon toward housing and reaches a parking lot/trail access point after 0.3 mile. The trail is somewhat steep but offers great views.

0.8 This access point is almost directly on the trail and very easy to find.

1.0 Reach another parking lot/access trail. (*Note:* This trail leads to Argyle Restaurant and could make a great end to the hike if you're looking for a meal or cocktail.)

1.6 After traveling through the lushest parts of the trail, reach the last parking lot/access point on the trail and your turnaround point. Return the way you came. (**Option:** Follow any of multiple other routes back to the trailhead.)

3.2 Arrive back at the trailhead.

Belmont Park Beach

One of two remaining wooden roller coasters in coastal California, the 1925 Giant Dipper rises above this wide beach and grassy park that is the heart of Mission Beach's beach scene and a must-do hike for people who love to people watch. You'll pass surf shops, custom bikini stores, and local fish taco hangouts and find lots of places to sit awhile and watch the world walk, bike, or skate by. You can't say you've been to San Diego if you haven't traversed this most interesting boardwalk.

Start: Far end parking lot on North Jetty Road or lower parking lot at Belmont Park Beach

Distance: 2.5 miles point to point

Approximate hiking time: 3 hours

Difficulty: Easy

Trail surface: Cement path, sandy beach

Best season: Summer, when the beach is at its most raucous

Other trail users: In-line skaters, joggers, strollers, kids, lots of people in beach attire

Canine compatibility: Leashed dogs allowed from 6:00 p.m. to 9:00 a.m. only (You must clean up after your pet.)

Fees and permits: No fees or permits required

Schedule: Open 24 hours daily

Maps: USGS La Jolla OEW

Trail contacts: City of San Diego, 202 C Street, MS #10A, San Diego, CA 92101; (619) 525-8213; www
.sandiego.gov/park-and-
recreation/parks/missionbay/
index.shtml

Special considerations: Bring a camera and add some cinema verité images to your collection.

Finding the trailhead: From I-5, take I-8 west toward the beaches (signed). Take the Mission Bay Drive exit, continuing west. Turn left (west) onto Mission Bay Drive and drive to the end of the street. Park in the far end parking area on North Jetty Road if you can find a spot. Otherwise park in the public parking area across the street from Belmont Park. GPS: N32.769 / W117.252

Mission Beach is old San Diego at its most crowded. The slim bit of land between the ocean and the bay is top real estate for beach lovers. The hike begins at the tip of Mission Beach, overlooking Ocean Beach across the river. This is one of the few areas left that allow beach fires, and if you're here at night, as you turn around to head north along the beach, you'll see many fire pits flaming. Watch where you are going, because the cement fire pits can be hard to see at night when they are not surrounded by partygoers.

For easier walking, hop up to Ocean Front Walk, a wide boardwalk that lines the beach all the way up through Pacific Beach. You'll observe a classic California beach scene straight out of *Beach Blanket Bingo*—wide, white sandy beaches, even waves, and scores of skaters, families, surfers, fishing enthusiasts, and couples.

This long stretch of beach is San Diego's most popular and attracts millions of visitors throughout the year. The crowds are part of the fun, and people watching may make you forget the fabulous view of the sea.

Begin your hike at the southernmost tip of Mission Beach and simply head north, favoring the packed wet sand along the water's edge or the more challenging dry sand a little farther inland. The beach quickly narrows, and you may enjoy gaping at the homes along this 2-block-wide strand as much as you enjoy the vistas of the sea.

Mist rises over Pacific Beach and Crystal Pier.

Belmont Park offers a large grassy lawn, plenty of parking, and a wooden roller coaster that celebrated its eighty-fifth anniversary in 2010, making it one of the oldest operating coasters in the world. It was restored in 1990, and other rides have been added to the park for those who want more modern thrills. It is a hoot to enjoy the Giant Dipper's rickety ride.

Take a moment to visit The Plunge, an Olympic-size pool that is always busy, since it serves as the local community pool. When built in 1925, it was the largest saltwater pool in the world, with 400,000 gallons of water underneath a light-filled roof. Designers eschewed the typical Art Deco design of the time to mirror the Spanish Renaissance–style buildings recently completed within Balboa Park. The pool reflects old-world luxury with its walls of dramatic arches surrounding a classic rectangular design topped off with a magnificent wall-to-wall-to-ceiling mural of orcas frolicking underwater. The Plunge's main function remains to teach people to swim, as it did Esther Williams, Johnny Weissmuller, and one million others. Since 1940, fresh water has replaced salt water.

Continue north to a broad street that feeds directly onto the beach, although cars are not allowed to go that far. This is classic Southern California, with surf shops, small restaurants that have been there forever, custom bikini shops, and places to rent in-line skates, bicycles, surfboards, and more. "The Dude" from *The Big Lebowski* would live here, if he could just find the money.

Keep heading north, enjoying the humanity until you reach Crystal Pier, offering cute cottages on the pier that can be rented by the day, week, or month in one of the most distinctive beachfront resorts in San Diego. Pacific Beach contains lots of upscale tattoo parlors, health food joints, and Thai restaurants within a classic yuppie beachfront community. This is where you'll pick up your ride or, if you are up to hiking back, return the way you came.

Option: From Crystal Pier, cross Mission Boulevard, which runs the length of Mission Beach, to enjoy the bayside part of the community. Since the strand is only 2 blocks wide south of Yarmouth Court, you can cut across at your discretion to enjoy Bayside Walk. At Mission Bay Drive you'll want to head straight south, unless your legs are willing to add another mile or so to your journey by following the outline of the inland peninsula. This will eventually lead back to Bonita Cove and Mariners Basin, which abut Belmont Park on the bay side. You can't really get lost if you follow the shoreline south—it eventually wanders back to the parking lot where you began.

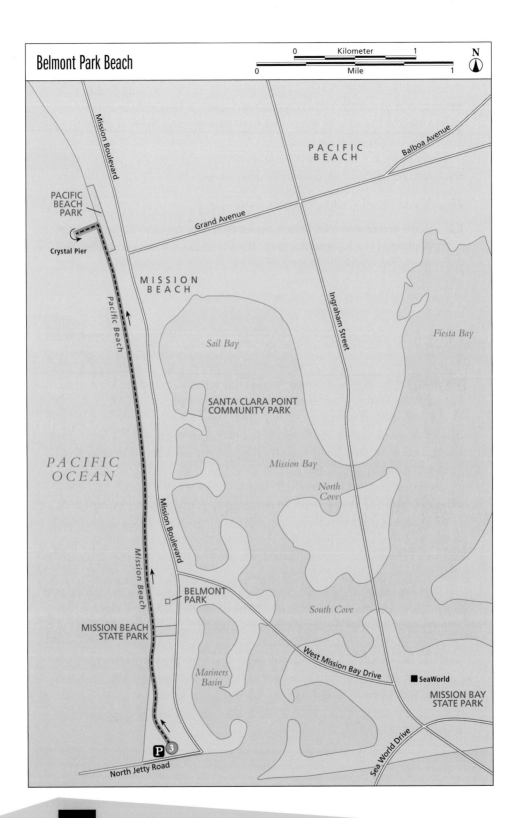

Belmont Park Beach

0 Kilometer 1
0 Mile 1

N

PACIFIC
BEACH

Balboa Avenue

Mission Boulevard

PACIFIC
BEACH
PARK

Grand Avenue

Crystal Pier

MISSION
BEACH

Ingraham Street

Sail Bay

Fiesta Bay

Pacific Beach

SANTA CLARA POINT
COMMUNITY PARK

Mission Bay

PACIFIC
OCEAN

North
Cove

Mission Boulevard

Mission Beach

South Cove

BELMONT
PARK

MISSION BEACH
STATE PARK

West Mission Bay Drive

SeaWorld

Mariners
Basin

MISSION BAY
STATE PARK

Sea World Drive

P 3

North Jetty Road

MILES AND DIRECTIONS

0.0   Start at the parking lot (if you can find a spot) on North Jetty Road.

0.3   Belmont Park Beachfront Amusement is worth an hour or so of shopping, rides, and games.

0.6   Mission Bay Drive ends at the beach.

2.0   Mission Beach melds into Pacific Beach.

2.5   At the end of your hike, Crystal Pier extends from the heart of Pacific Beach. (**Option:** If you haven't arranged for a shuttle, turn around and head back to the trailhead for a 5.0-mile round-trip.)

The graceful arc of the vibrant wooden coaster contrasts with the gray sky.

4

Coronado Ferry

After taking a ferry to Coronado Landing Park, walk along the harbor to observe scenic San Diego Bay with the sparkling city as a backdrop. Wander along the shoreline until you reach Tidelands Park, a multiuse park complete with sandy beach, whimsical public art, and grassy fields, all hiding in the shadow of the magnificent Coronado Bay Bridge.

Start: Coronado Landing Park ferry landing
Distance: 3.6 miles out and back
Approximate hiking time: 2 hours
Difficulty: Easy
Trail surface: Paved
Best season: Year-round
Other trail users: Cyclists, strollers, strolling minstrels, skaters, bathers, tourists
Canine compatibility: Leashed dogs allowed. (You must clean up after your pet.)
Fees and permits: No fees or permits required
Schedule: Tidelands Park open 6:00 a.m. to 10:30 p.m.

Maps: USGS Point Loma; trail map available online at www.californiacoastaltrail.info/hikers/hikers_main_horizontal.php?DisplayAction=DisplaySection&CountyId=21&SectionId=405
Trail contacts: Unified Port of San Diego, 3165 Pacific Hwy., San Diego, CA 92101; (619) 686-6200
Ferry Landing, 1201 First St., Suite 6, Coronado, CA 92118; (619) 435-8895
Tidelands Park, Mullinex Drive at Glorietta Boulevard, Coronado, CA 92118; (619) 686-6225

Finding the trailhead: By car, from I-5 take the Coronado Bay Bridge exit. Take the first right after crossing the bridge onto Glorietta Boulevard. Glorietta curves left and becomes Second Street. Follow Second Street to B Avenue, which feeds into the ferry landing. (You may have a hard time finding a parking space, so take advantage of any spot you find.) GPS: N32.699886 / W117.170048

By water from San Diego, board the ferry at Broadway Pier; the ferry runs hourly from 9:00 a.m. to 10:00 p.m. Water taxis also are available; call (619) 235-8294 for pickup.

THE HIKE

Ferry service from the mainland near Market Street to Coronado Island began almost as soon as Babcock and Story purchased the island in 1886. The team immediately began construction of the Hotel del Coronado, and tourists eagerly flocked to the island for rest and recreation. When the swooping 2.12-mile-long Coronado Bay Bridge opened in 1969, many thought ferry service would soon become a thing of the past. But downtown San Diego reinvented itself after Horton Plaza was built in the 1980s, going from an area of seedy peepshows and tattoo parlors to one of the hottest downtown destinations on the California coast. Visitors drawn to the vibrant nightlife and residents of new upscale condos soon reinvigorated the ferry service. Many downtown condo dwellers leave their cars in their parking lots or garages and take the ferry on a leisurely excursion across the bay, where they can wander on foot to restaurants, shopping, and nearby parks.

This is a particularly beautiful twilight hike, when you can watch lights begin to flicker on across the harbor like Western fireflies. Begin at the ferry landing, which offers restaurants, shopping and alternative modes of transportation, and head left along the bayside walk. (**Option:** Immediately west of the landing is Centennial Park, a pretty little green area with its own sandy beach. Many people enjoy wandering through the park before heading off along the bayfront walk.)

The trail mostly follows the Bayside Bikeway from the ferry landing to Tidelands Park and features breathtaking views of downtown San Diego and the underbelly

Old Ferry Landing Shopping Center is located just off the pier.

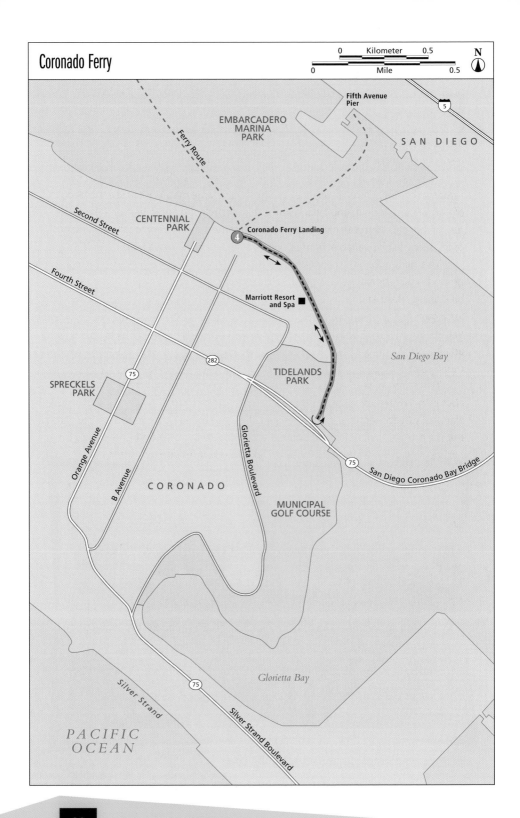

Coronado Ferry

0 Kilometer 0.5
0 Mile 0.5

N

Fifth Avenue Pier

EMBARCADERO MARINA PARK

Ferry Route

SAN DIEGO

5

Second Street

CENTENNIAL PARK

Coronado Ferry Landing

4

Fourth Street

Marriott Resort and Spa

San Diego Bay

282

75

SPRECKELS PARK

TIDELANDS PARK

Orange Avenue

B Avenue

Glorietta Boulevard

CORONADO

MUNICIPAL GOLF COURSE

75

San Diego Coronado Bay Bridge

75

Glorietta Bay

Silver Strand

Silver Strand Boulevard

PACIFIC OCEAN

of the Coronado Bay Bridge. There are numerous opportunities to get off the bike path and walk along sandy beaches or over grassy lawns, but often the bike path is the only walkable area. This is prime commercial property and features many top-of-the-line restaurants offering stunning views of the bay and the city, as well as the luxurious Marriott Resort and Spa. Stay along the water's edge, or explore the resort's well-landscaped property, as the island curves and the path turns due south.

Tidelands Park butts up against the resort property and offers whimsical sculptures that capture the bike-bay theme. Stop by the large map kiosk to see the layout of Port of San Diego hiking/biking paths that encircle the entire harbor. Take a picture of the map with your cell phone or digital camera if you want to take advantage of the many hikes available; printed copies of the map are unavailable.

This hike ends at the twenty-two-acre Tidelands Park, which offers a playground, a skateboard park, four ball fields, exercise stations, a gazebo, picnic tables, bike and pedestrian paths, bike parking, a public fishing pier, and a large parking lot. However, the path continues to Hotel del Coronado, using existing streets to fill in the gaps. (If you drive to this hike, consider reversing the order so that you take advantage of the park's excellent parking facilities.) The park's beach is a favorite of mothers with small children, since waves and tides are minimal.

The entire hike offers wonderful views of the bridge, which soars 200 feet above the water to accommodate the hefty military ships that head down to National City for repair and maintenance. It is rare to look over at the bridge and not see a white sail as pleasure boaters and sailors swing back and forth across the harbor. Return the way you came after dipping your toes into the water.

MILES AND DIRECTIONS

0.0   Start at the ferry landing, heading left as you face Coronado.

0.1   Find the bike path that follows the line between the sand and the sea.

0.5   Note the beautiful grounds of the Marriott Resort and Spa.

0.7   Enter Tidelands Park, enjoying the sculptures along the path.

0.9   Spend some time studying the Port of San Diego parks and paths on the map kiosk.

1.0   Many kayakers depart from this calm beach area. Watch out for toddlers.

1.8   Head down to the beach before turning around and hiking back to the ferry.

3.6   Arrive back at the ferry landing.

Hotel Del Coronado Beach Walk

This walk begins at the fence that restricts casual visitors from North Island and heads south past one of the most historic buildings in San Diego—the magnificent Hotel del Coronado—before meandering south. Enjoy views of Mexico and the distant islands as you walk along one of California's most classic beaches.

Start: Beach access stairs at the corner of Ocean Drive and Ocean Boulevard

Distance: 1.8 miles out and back

Approximate hiking time: 1–2 hours

Difficulty: Easy

Trail surface: Sand

Best season: Year-round

Other trail users: Beachcombers, surfers, kids with pails, millionaires, soldiers in training storming the beach

Canine compatibility: No dogs allowed

Fees and permits: No fees or permits required

Schedule: Sunrise to sunset

Maps: USGS Point Loma; trail map available online at www .californiacoastaltrail.info/hikers/ hikers_main_horizontal.php? DisplayAction=DisplaySection& CountyId=21&SectionId=405

Trail contacts: City of Coronado, 1825 Strand Way, Coronado, CA 92118; (619) 522-7300

Finding the trailhead: From I-5 cross over the Coronado Bay Bridge into Coronado. Continue until you hit Orange Avenue. Turn left onto Orange and then right onto Ocean Boulevard. Follow Ocean Boulevard along the shoreline until you hit Ocean Drive. Park where you can find a spot, then cross over to the beach and head along the beach away from the military base. GPS: N32.687 / W117.191

THE HIKE

he island of Coronado and the Hotel del Coronado have been inextricably linked since the hotel's construction. News of the upcoming hotel brought workers, who built houses and the surrounding community. By the time the hotel was completed in 1888, the small community was thriving.

The distinctive hotel was an immediate hit, drawing families, foreigners, and the famous to frolic on the wide, white beaches; watch the whales skim by; and test the winds with flying machines. Charles Lindbergh tested the newly constructed *Spirit of St. Louis,* built in San Diego, from the north end of the island. When he returned after his famous cross-Atlantic flight, he celebrated at the hotel; Will Rogers was the emcee.

North Island was soon known for its aviation adventures, and in 1911 the local flight school trained the Navy's first pilot. By 1912 the Navy had established its winter headquarters on North Island. The military and tourism from the hotel and beaches have defined Coronado ever since.

Our hike begins at the edge of the field that divides North Island Naval Air Station and the public beach. Wire fences and a guarded gate at the end of Ocean Boulevard clearly delineate the line between the two. Head away from the air station, but don't be surprised if a U.S. Navy jet flies over your head, the belly of the plane clearly visible from the ground. Looking south, the deep pink cones that float atop the white wood Victorian-style Hotel del Coronado can be clearly seen in the

Point Loma looms in the distance against the white sands of Coronado.

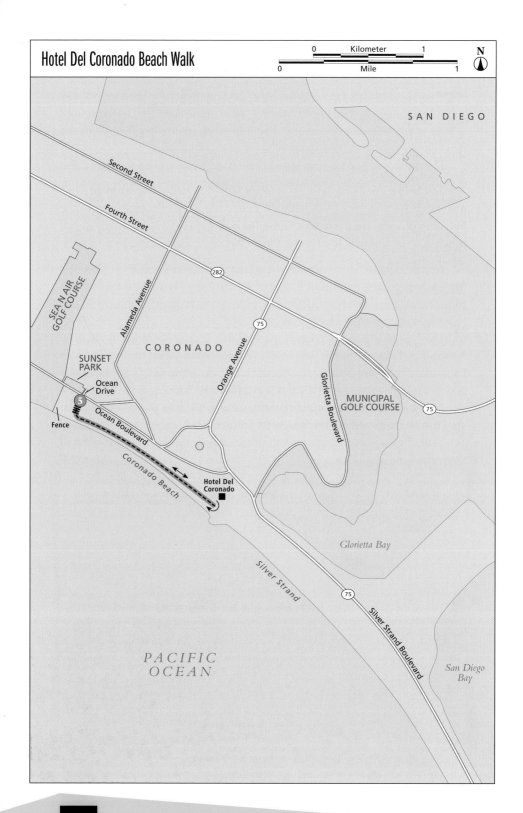

Hotel Del Coronado Beach Walk

SAN DIEGO

Second Street

Fourth Street

SEA N AIR GOLF COURSE

282

75

CORONADO

Alameda Avenue

Orange Avenue

SUNSET PARK

Ocean Drive

5

Fence

Ocean Boulevard

Glorietta Boulevard

MUNICIPAL GOLF COURSE

75

Coronado Beach

Hotel Del Coronado

Glorietta Bay

Silver Strand

75

PACIFIC OCEAN

Silver Strand Boulevard

San Diego Bay

N

0   Kilometer   1

0   Mile   1

distance. This is the hotel where Tony Curtis wooed Marilyn Monroe in *Some Like It Hot*. It is also where L. Frank Baum wrote *The Wizard of Oz*.

As you stroll toward the hotel, you'll encounter many beach lovers along the way. Coronado Beach is the widest in Southern California and draws the usual sand-and-saltwater-loving crowd. Stephen "Dr. Beach" Leatherman, Director of Florida International University's Laboratory for Coastal Research, has rated the beach the third best in the United States.

Just before you get to the hotel, note the large Coronado sculpted in the sand, mimicking the long-gone sand dunes. Be sure to take a few minutes to wander the hotel complex and see the historic lobby. The walk from the hotel out to the broad beach is an excursion in itself. Enjoy the ambience, the upscale patrons, and the family-friendly atmosphere before heading back north.

MILES AND DIRECTIONS

0.0　Start at the corner of Ocean Drive and Ocean Boulevard at the beach access stairs.

0.9　Walk by the distinctive red spires of Hotel del Coronado. Enjoy the hotel's Victorian ambience and beautiful beach before turning around and heading back north. (**Option:** Continuing south you'll pass a few high-rise condos before entering the beach side of another Navy complex, the Naval Amphibious Base. The area is off-limits, but if you look south you might see a group of Navy SEALs storming the beach as part of their training. If you want to continue south, you'll have to cross over to the bay side of the island. It's not too tough to do, and the walk is definitely worth the effort.)

1.8　Arrive back at the trailhead.

Coronado has been a military town since 1913, when the U.S. Army established a presence here. The U.S. Navy air station soon followed and took over the north end of the island. North Island is currently home to three aircraft carriers and many fighter planes. The south end houses the renowned Navy SEALs and some of the most coveted military housing in the country.

Point Loma Tide Pools

Tucked away on the western edge of the peninsula, this short hike takes you along the gorgeous coastline that serves as one of the area's most important ecosystems. The trail wanders close to the cliff and offers the opportunity to scramble down to visit tide pools, do a little nature observation, and then clamber back to wander along one of the most remote promontories in Southern California.

Start: First public parking lot just past the U.S. Navy base

Distance: 0.9 mile out and back

Approximate hiking time: 30 minutes

Difficulty: Easy

Trail surface: Sand, dirt path

Best season: Year-round

Other trail users: Biologists, students

Canine compatibility: Leashed dogs allowed, but only on this path

Fees and permits: Parking fee or national park pass

Schedule: Park open 9:00 a.m. to 5:00 p.m. For security purposes, the entrance station closes at 4:30 p.m., and the main gate into Cabrillo National Monument is closed at 4:45 p.m. All visitors must exit the park by 5:00 p.m.

Maps: USGS Point Loma; trail map available online at www .nps.gov/cabr/planyourvisit/ loader.cfm?csModule=security/ getfile&PageID=21254

Trail contacts: Cabrillo National Monument, 1800 Cabrillo Memorial Dr., San Diego, CA 92106; (619) 557-5450; www.nps.gov/cabr

Special concerns: Do not walk along the road to the parking lot.

Finding the trailhead: Located on Point Loma, Cabrillo National Monument is within the San Diego city limits. Take I-8 west to the Rosecrans Street/Highway 209 exit, then travel about 2.5 miles before turning right onto Canon Street. Next turn left onto Catalina Boulevard and follow the signs to the park. After paying the parking fee, follow the road all the way down to the right. Park in the first lot. GPS: N32.668278 / W117.244294

THE HIKE

Life in tide pools is dictated by the ceaseless rise and fall of the ocean, and the interesting creatures you'll find here have adapted to this rare and fascinating environment. You'll notice how dense and small the ecosystem is, with many different types of creature living side by side. Anemones, octopuses, dead man's fingers, and starfish can all be seen wedged into the rocks in these shallow pools.

This is a great hike to take with your kids. Children are fascinated by the small worlds enclosed within the shallow pools. Most creatures can be touched very gently, but make sure not to squeeze, pry, move, or apply force to an animal. Ask a park ranger for tips on enjoying the tide pools, including what can and cannot be touched. A Junior Ranger program is offered at the visitor center.

The rocks are often slippery and wet, so wear shoes with good traction and avoid running. The trail is short and follows a gradual grade uphill. Rangers ask that you do not walk along the narrow, twisty road down to the parking lot.

In the late 1800s, when the Point Loma Lighthouse was still occupied, the lighthouse keeper's children rowed themselves to school each day from Point Loma to Old Town, across the bay.

From this upper vantage point, you command a wide view of the tide pools and southernmost tip of Point Loma.

Point Loma Tide Pools

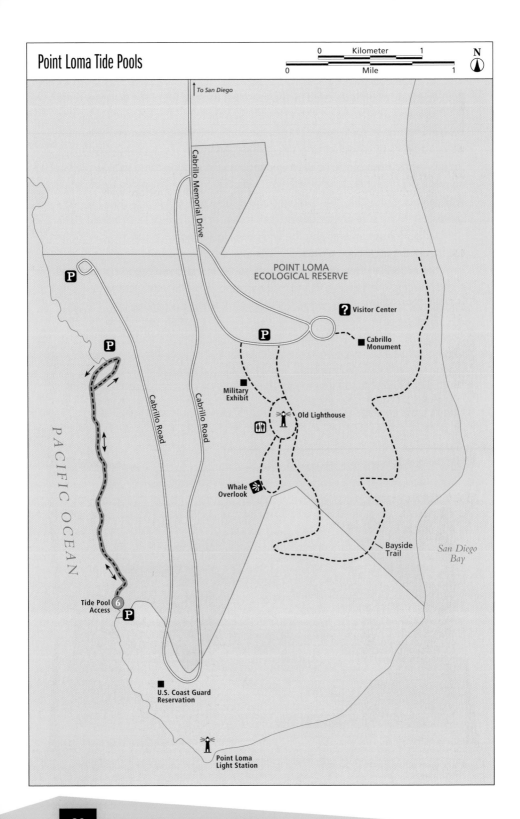

Kilometer
0 — 1

Mile
0 — 1

N

To San Diego

Cabrillo Memorial Drive

POINT LOMA
ECOLOGICAL RESERVE

P

Visitor Center

Cabrillo
Monument

P

Military
Exhibit

Cabrillo Road

Cabrillo Road

P

PACIFIC OCEAN

Old Lighthouse

Whale
Overlook

Bayside
Trail

San Diego
Bay

Tide Pool 6
Access

P

U.S. Coast Guard
Reservation

Point Loma
Light Station

0.0   Start at the lower parking lot. Enjoy the gentle ocean breeze as you take the path heading north along the coastline.

0.1   The first tide pool appears on your left. Enjoy the mysteries within.

0.4   Arrive at another easily accessible tide pool. Take a few minutes to enjoy it. Turn around to head back toward the trailhead. (**Option:** Walk another tenth of a mile up the hill to a lookout point. Walk back downhill and rejoin the trail.)

0.9   Arrive back at the trailhead.

Abalone, once common in Point Loma's tide pools, has been overharvested to the point that it is rarely found today. The same fate could befall the owl limpet, another gastropod that is harvested for food. The owl limpets at Point Loma are protected within the national park and are therefore larger and more numerous than even a few miles away at Sunset Cliffs. However, between 1990 and 1995 the number of owl limpets dropped by 23 percent overall and were found to be 5.25 mm smaller than they once were. Unfortunately, poachers still harvest owl limpets in Point Loma despite its illegality, threatening to destroy the entire population, because owl limpets are born male and only become female when they get older and larger.

A sign warns visitors to be wary of unstable cliff edges.

San Diego Port

Wander along the heart of San Diego Port, which once was a major fishing as well as military port. The walk along the bay features a maritime museum with tall ships, military ships, statues, and memorials that recognize San Diego's impressive maritime history. Continue to Seaport Village for shopping, dining, and great views across the harbor. End with a spectacular vista from the top of the convention center.

Start: Harbor Drive

Distance: 4.6 miles out and back

Approximate hiking time: 2 hours

Difficulty: Moderate due to length

Trail surface: Sidewalk

Best season: Year-round

Other trail users: Joggers, bike-taxies, tourists, sailors

Canine compatibility: Leashed dogs allowed. (You must clean up after your pet.)

Fees and permits: No fees or permits required to enter port, but bring quarters for parking

Schedule: Open 24 hours

Maps: USGS Point Loma; trail map available at www.co.san-diego.ca.us/reusable_components/images/parks/doc/Trails_OVRP.pdf

Trail contacts: Unified Port of San Diego, 3165 Pacific Hwy., San Diego, CA 92101; (619) 686-6200

Maritime Museum of San Diego, 1492 North Harbor Dr., San Diego, CA 92101; (619) 234-9153; www.sdmaritime.org

Finding the trailhead: From I-5 take the Laurel Street exit, heading west toward the harbor. Turn left (south) onto Harbor Drive. Park at Hawthorn or Grape Street or as soon as you can find a space along Harbor Drive. There are parking areas all along the street before you get to the big ships. GPS: N32.725099 / W117.173706

THE HIKE

San Diego has so many assets, from its striking vistas to its balmy weather to its superb beaches, that we often forget why Europeans first settled in the area. It was one of the first places Europeans landed on what is now U.S. soil. Early whalers made San Diego a port where they not only caught the California gray whale but also processed their kills.

Even after whalers retired from San Diego Harbor, the port remained a major fishing destination. Fishing boats launched from San Diego and traveled throughout the world catching primarily tuna, which they brought back home to process. The "Tuna Capital of the World" hosted the world's largest tuna fleet from the 1930s to the 1970s, and each evening you could sit at one of the local waterfront restaurants to watch the fleet come in.

First Chinese immigrants in the second half of the nineteenth century and then Italian, Portuguese, and Japanese fishermen settled in the area, which employed up to 40,000 people in the tuna fishing, canning, and processing industry, San Diego's third largest at the time. Famous local companies included Starkist, Bumblebee, and Van Camp Seafood. In the late 1970s the industry sailed away to foreign shores, where labor was cheaper and standards less stringent. Seaport Village features a number of seafood restaurants that still get their seafood daily from the 200 boats that remain in the fishing fleet.

From its prime location, the San Diego Convention Center overlooks both the harbor and the historic Gaslamp Quarter.

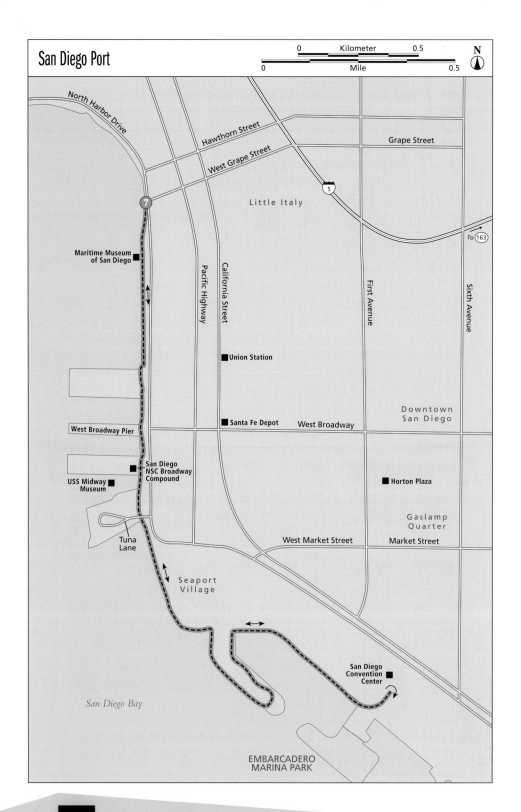

San Diego Port

0 — Kilometer — 0.5
0 — Mile — 0.5

N

North Harbor Drive

Hawthorn Street

West Grape Street

Grape Street

Little Italy

5

To 163

Maritime Museum
of San Diego

Pacific Highway

California Street

First Avenue

Sixth Avenue

Union Station

Downtown
San Diego

West Broadway Pier

Santa Fe Depot

West Broadway

San Diego
NSC Broadway
Compound

USS Midway
Museum

Horton Plaza

Gaslamp
Quarter

Tuna
Lane

West Market Street

Market Street

Seaport
Village

San Diego
Convention
Center

San Diego Bay

EMBARCADERO
MARINA PARK

Begin the walk by heading south along the harbor. You'll go by one of the largest collections of historic tall ships in the world, collected by the Maritime Museum of San Diego. To many, the *Star of India* is the symbol of San Diego. The city's first historic vessel sits like a queen in the harbor. Built on the Isle of Man in 1863, it is the oldest active sailing ship in the world. You'll also walk by the *San Salvador,* a replica of Juan Rodríguez Cabrillo's flagship vessel, which was the first ship to explore the western coast of the United States. The HMS *Surprise* is a replica of the twenty-four-gun eighteenth-century Royal Navy frigate *Rose*. The *Californian* was acquired by the museum in 2002. The sailing vessel was built in 1984 and launched at the summer Olympic Games in Los Angeles. In July 2003 the governor designated the *Californian* as the Official Tall Ship of California.

The B-39 submarine showcases a war vessel from a more modern era. This Soviet submarine served from the 1970s to the end of the Cold War. Decommissioned from the Soviet navy in 1995, it was purchased by a consortium from Vancouver. In 2002 it was relocated to Seattle, finally moving to San Diego in 2004. The *SD Harbor Pilot* was the main pilot boat from 1914 to 1996, leading commercial ships into and out of the harbor.

Continue to the port where cruise ships load and unload passengers, and where you can catch a ferry to see the bay. The USS Midway Museum, housed on the longest-serving Navy aircraft carrier in the twentieth century, features other historical artifacts and information. There are twenty-five restored aircraft on the historic carrier. After reaching the port, continue walking along the harbor.

(*Option:* Take the side excursion into Tuna Lane. The Fish Market restaurant offers stunning views of the harbor and sculptures placed at various points around the building. As you leave the loop and continue along the bay, you'll see a set of memorials for San Diego's lost military heroes. Keep hugging the harbor line until you get to Seaport Village, a collection of shops, restaurants, and amusements. One of the area's most popular local seafood spots, The Pier Cafe sits on the water and offers fabulous views as well as wonderful seafood direct from the boats. Continue following the coast for a scenic loop with great views of Coronado.)

At the end of the man-made bay on the land side, the San Diego Convention Center offers sculptural stairs that travel over the top of the building. Take a moment to view downtown, the harbor, Coronado Island, and even Mexico from the building's promontory. Turn around and head back to your car.

MILES AND DIRECTIONS

0.0 Start from one of the parking areas along the harbor and head south.

0.5 Pass the tall ships and military museums along the harbor, including the large aircraft carrier that is the fascinating USS Midway Museum, a delightful attraction in itself.

0.6 Note the cruise ships, if any are in dock.

1.1 Cut straight across the peninsula as it juts out. (**Option:** Take a jaunt out to the end of the finger and then return to the same path.)

1.6 Pass by Seaport Village. Take a walk along the bay to check out Tuna Harbor.

2.3 Ascend the convention center stairs to check out the city. Turn around and retrace your steps toward the trailhead. (**Option:** Cross over the convention center to loop around through Gaslamp Quarter, turning left on Broadway to get back to the USS *Midway* where you will turn north to find your car.)

4.6 Arrive back at the trailhead.

How Green Is My Tuna?

All is not lost in the tuna-fishing industry. Fishing tour boats depart from various locations along San Diego's harbor, allowing you to experience the thrill of catching your own tuna the old-fashioned way—with a pole and line.

Six local San Diego fishing families recently came together to create American Tuna, featuring pole-caught (no nets) surface tuna "caught by American fishermen in American waters, delivered to American ports, canned in America, and intended for American consumers." The dolphin-friendly fishing method and the cooked-once process make the product a favorite of green groups and gourmet cooks, as well as sustainable fishing organizations such as the Monterey Aquarium and Seafood Watch.

Shelter Island

Shelter Island is known primarily for its yacht club, restaurants, and hotels. This linear park borders the bay side of the small island and looks across to North Island, with its impressive military ships. This is one of the best locations for watching San Diego's many sailing events, such as the annual Festival of Sail.

Start: Begin at the southwest tip of the island

Distance: 2.0 miles out and back

Approximate hiking time: 45 minutes

Difficulty: Easy

Trail surface: Paved

Best season: Year-round

Other trail users: Anglers, tourists, sailors swimming ashore

Canine compatibility: Leashed dogs allowed

Fees and permits: No fees or permits required

Schedule: Sunrise to sunset

Maps: USGS Point Loma; trail map available online at www .californiacoastaltrail.info/hikers/ hikers_main_horizontal.php? DisplayAction=DisplaySection& CountyId=21&SectionId=405

Trail contacts: Unified Port of San Diego, 3165 Pacific Hwy., San Diego, CA 92101; (619) 686-6200
Harbor Island Park, San Diego, CA; (619) 323-3101; www.portof sandiego.org/harbor-island-park .html

Finding the trailhead: Take I-5 (north or south) or I-8 west to the Rosecrans/ CA 209 exit and then continue west on CA 209. Drive 2.5 miles and turn left onto Shelter Island Drive. Go to the west end of the island and park in the lot or in one of the parking areas bordering the park. The trailhead is located at the tip of the island. GPS: N32.70821 / W117.234528

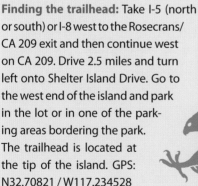

The first man-made "island" in San Diego Harbor was Shelter Island, which was built up over decades when the federal government and the San Diego Harbor Commission dredged a 200-foot-wide channel to accommodate military ships. At the same time, they dredged a channel to the San Diego Yacht Club clubhouse. The mudflat got the extra dirt, and eventually it rose high enough to remain permanently above water.

A small battle ensued over the use of the new landmass. Some wanted a place to picnic and fish; others wanted more sophisticated amenities like the clubhouse and additional resorts. Harbormaster John Bates decided to let both groups have their way, creating a linear park that lines the bay side of the island and leaving plenty of room on the land side to host a marina, motels, and restaurants. During the 1930s, the club began hosting yacht races and soon had an international reputation in racing circles. In the 1950s, city planners built a causeway out to the island, and its reputation as a playground for the sailing crowd and a favorite destination for picnics and fishing was assured.

The tuna industry greatly contributed to the growth of San Diego.

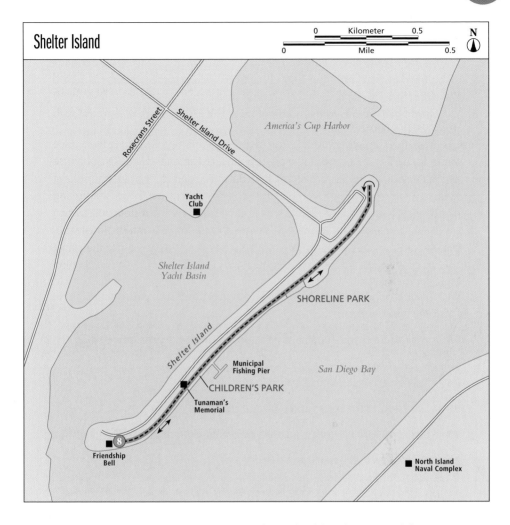

Shelter Island

Start your walk at the western end of the island, heading toward the water's edge. The island is known for its sculptures, the first of which will be found at Pacific Rim Park. *Pearl of the Pacific,* by San Diego artist James Hubbell, features a round ball floating in water surrounded by mosaic sea monsters.

Head across the road to the small shelter in the center of a grassy area. The Japanese-style pagoda houses the Friendship Bell, created by Masahiko Katori of Japan and presented to the city in 1958 by the citizens of Yokohama to celebrate the two cities' new Sister City relationship, the first such connection on the West Coast. Head back to the water's edge to look across the bay to North Island. This is as close as you will get to the military airfield. Typically one or two large aircraft carriers are berthed alongside the base.

8

About halfway down the park, take a moment to observe the brawny Tunaman's Memorial, honoring San Diego's commercial fishing history, before enjoying the antics of children at the adjacent, whimsical children's park. Take a quick stroll out on the fishing pier, where you can get refreshments at Sharkey's. Continue along the park path, scooting around the beach and boat launching area, where the grass seems to run out.

Keep heading toward the northern tip of the island, continuing to the right if you want to watch boats in action and on the left bank if you want to lust after yacht after yacht as they sit in the dock of the bay.

Stop for a cocktail at Bali Hai Restaurant, where you can watch the occasional dolphin frolic in the water or kayaker glide past, before returning the way you came.

MILES AND DIRECTIONS

0.0   Start at the tip of the island on the water's edge and head northeast to the grassy lawn.

0.1   Walk around the Friendship Bell and then return to the park running along the water's edge.

0.4   Walk around the Tunaman's Memorial, imagining yourself catching the fish.

0.6   Take an excursion onto the fishing pier.

0.8   Skirt around the beach and boat launch area.

1.0   Stop into Bali Hai's for a cool drink before heading back the way you came.

2.0   Arrive back at the trailhead.

Each September, San Diego hosts YachtFest (www.yachtfest.com), a sailing event that features superyachts and a mock gun battle between two tall ship replicas from the collection of the Maritime Museum of San Diego.

Sunset Cliffs

Between Hillside Park and Ladera Street along Sunset Cliffs Road, the high cliffs offer one of the most breathtaking and popular walks in San Diego—especially at sunset, when the sun reflects off the water in all its glory.

Start: Sunset Cliffs Park parking lot. Explore the park before heading north along the cliffs.
Distance: 1.6 miles point to point
Approximate hiking time: 1 leisurely hour
Difficulty: Easy
Trail surface: Dirt path, sidewalk, wooden and cement stairs
Best season: Year-round
Other trail users: Lovers, photographers, old ladies and gents
Canine compatibility: Leashed dogs allowed
Fees and permits: No fees or permits required

Schedule: Open 24 hours
Maps: USGS Point Loma OEW; trail map available online at www .californiacoastaltrail.info/hikers/ hikers_main_horizontal.php? DisplayAction=DisplaySection& CountyId=21&SectionId=402
Trail contacts: San Diego Parks and Recreation, Shoreline Parks, 2125 Park Blvd., San Diego, CA 92101; (619) 235-1169
Special considerations: Catch the cliffs at sunset for a startlingly beautiful view.

Finding the trailhead: From I-5, take I-8 west toward the beaches, following the signs for Sunset Cliffs. Follow Sunset Cliffs Boulevard for 2.5 miles until the road almost goes off the cliffs at Hillside Park. Find a parking space and begin to walk. (*Note:* We started our hike from the top of the cliffs at Hillside Park.) GPS: N32.7191 / W117.255

THE HIKE

Sunset Cliffs Natural Park looks like a narrow (very narrow) strip of land between the road and the edge of the fragile sandstone cliffs between Ocean Beach and Point Loma. The view from these hills is so striking, however, that each evening hundreds of people drop everything to walk along the edge of the cliffs to watch the sun go down.

The sixty-eight-acre park borders the rim of Point Loma and connects with the 640-acre Point Loma Ecological Reserve, which extends into the Navy property that covers the tip of Point Loma. Red coastal bluffs, arches, sea caves, sandy promontories, and sandstone gorges provide views that span deep into the horizon of the Pacific Ocean. Migratory whales, endangered pelicans, and sea lions all enjoy this stretch of ocean, whose waves make it less hospitable to humans. Beaches here are narrow, transient, and often enclosed in small, isolated coves that are nearly impossible to reach from land. Along the walk, the city has constructed a few sets of sturdy stairs going down to some of the larger beach areas, but even these beaches are often too narrow to navigate.

People climb along the cliff edges, but there is a reason there are warning notices posted all along the walkway. The sandy cliffs are extremely unstable. The surface may be slippery after a rain or ready to break off without notice. Clamber over the turtle guard at your own risk.

Couples, families, and teens flock to Sunset Cliffs to watch the sun dip below the horizon.

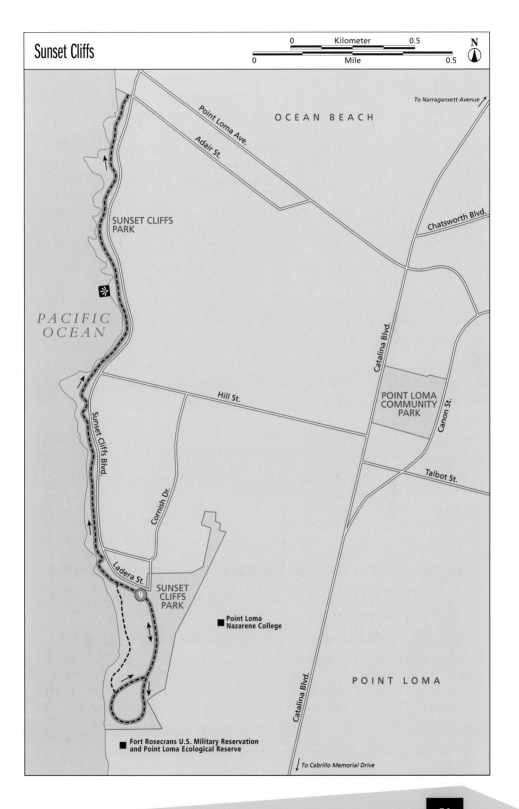

Kilometer

Mile

N

OCEAN BEACH

To Narragansett Avenue

Point Loma Ave.

Adair St.

Chatsworth Blvd.

SUNSET CLIFFS
PARK

PACIFIC
OCEAN

Catalina Blvd.

Hill St.

POINT LOMA
COMMUNITY
PARK

Canon St.

Sunset Cliffs Blvd.

Talbot St.

Cornish Dr.

Ladera St.

SUNSET
CLIFFS
PARK

Point Loma
Nazarene College

Catalina Blvd.

POINT LOMA

Fort Rosecrans U.S. Military Reservation
and Point Loma Ecological Reserve

To Cabrillo Memorial Drive

For a leg-burning option, hike up Hill Street, about midway along the hike. Point Loma begins to narrow at this point, and Hill takes you up to the peak of the landmass, offering a spectacular view of the ocean. It feels more like a vertical climb than a hike, but the houses, the breeze, and the burn are worth it.

Sunset Cliffs Park was dedicated in 1983, although people had long made the trek to the bluffs for the nightly lightshow. The hike begins at the fifty-acre Hillside Park, a natural open space that provides a place for people to play with their dogs off-leash and for those with vertigo to watch a sunset without standing on the precipice of a 50-foot-high cliff.

As you head north, you leave the park and walk along the rim of the continent. The weathered hills have been softened by wind and rain and exhibit enticing fingers of land that reach out toward the sea. Hikers often scramble out onto these promontories to sit in relative solitude as the world goes by behind them. Rangers ask that you stay on paths, however, not just for your own safety but also for the health of the fragile plants that cling to the delicate hills.

The park ends at Adair Street, where you can pick up your shuttle or turn around and head back the way you came for a 3.2-mile round-trip.

MILES AND DIRECTIONS

0.0 Start at the parking lot of Sunset Cliffs Park/Hillside Park on Ladera Street.

0.1 Explore the path heading south, which takes you to the old softball park overlooking the sea. Enjoy the gamboling dogs.

0.2 Head back north along the cliffs, scrambling up and down the gorge, or stay along the road for an easier walk.

0.3 Go right, past the parking lot.

0.4 Pass a sign indicating that restoration is in progress to maintain the site.

0.5 The trail meets up with the road. (**Option:** Take the stairway down to the beach and back.)

1.0 Enjoy the wide lookout.

1.6 Arrive at Adair Street and pick up your ride. (**Option:** Return the way you came for a 3.2-mile round-trip.)

Sweetwater Regional Park

This urban retreat centers around the Sweetwater Reservoir, offering backcountry mountains, a freshwater lake, and a surprising amount of wildlife. The area was once a hotspot for equestrians, and it is still common to find horses and their riders along the trails. Equally common now are golf carts, which travel within Bonita Golf Club, around which the park's paths wind.

Start: Equestrian staging area at the intersection of Sweetwater and Briarwood Roads
Distance: 2.4 miles out and back
Approximate hiking time: 1 hour
Difficulty: Easy
Trail surface: Dirt path, sidewalk
Best season: Year-round
Other trail users: Equestrians, mountain bikers, naturalists
Canine compatibility: Licensed dogs allowed on a 6-foot or shorter leash
Fees and permits: No fees or permits required

Schedule: Park open 9:30 a.m. to sunset
Maps: USGS National City; trail map available online at www .co.san-diego.ca.us/reusable_ components/images/parks/doc/ Trails_Sweetwater.pdf
Trail contacts: Sweetwater Regional Park, 3218 Summit Meadow Rd., Bonita, CA 91902; (877) 565-3600, (619) 472-7572, or (858) 565-3600 (local); www .sdparks.org

Finding the trailhead: Head toward South County on I-805 south and exit onto Sweetwater Road, traveling east. You'll see the park and hiking trails on the right. Continue to Briarwood Road and pull into the parking area. Start at the staging area and head away from the road, looking for the path toward the pond. All the trails from the parking lot meet with the east–west path. GPS: N32.67476 / W117.02405

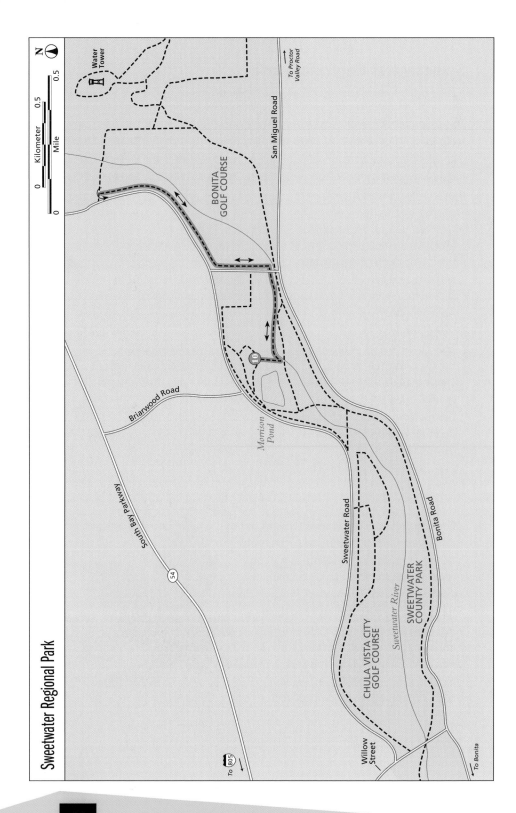

N

Water
Tower

Kilometer
0   0.5

Mile
0   0.5

To Proctor
Valley Road

San Miguel Road

BONITA
GOLF COURSE

Briarwood Road

Morrison
Pond

South Bay Parkway

54

Sweetwater Road

Sweetwater River

CHULA VISTA CITY
GOLF COURSE

SWEETWATER
COUNTY PARK

Bonita Road

Willow
Street

805
To 805

To Bonita

O ne of the county's top camping and equestrian spots, this 540-acre urban retreat offers 15 miles of trails and stunning views that take in everything from the sprawling hills of Tijuana to the rugged mountain of Mount Miguel to the east. But it isn't just campers who flock to the area. Joggers, families, teens, and lovers all enjoy strolling along the extensive trails that weave in and around the scenic reservoir and golf course. Hiking and equestrian trails lead through Summit Meadows, acres of grasslands, chaparral, and riverside wetlands.

The Sweetwater River and its surrounding valley encompass the town of Bonita. Horse properties were once common throughout the area, and a developer whose children showed horses made sure he included extensive bridal paths throughout the community.

Although the horse population has diminished, the network of trails remains. Don't be surprised to find yourself walking past the elegant creatures, with their favorite guide in the saddle. If you are unfamiliar with horses, make sure that you are cautious when passing. Even the most well-trained horse can be startled, and 1,200 pounds of muscle, bone, teeth, and hooves can do serious injury.

This elevated highway creates a dramatic overhead view near the dam at Sweetwater Regional Park.

0.0   Head east from the staging area at the intersection of Briarwood and Sweetwater Roads.

0.5   The path curves left; follow Bonita Road.

0.6   The path leads under a bridge.

0.9   Pass Bonita Golf Course.

1.2   The path leads to small set of corrals to your right. Have some fun watching the horses for a bit, then retrace your steps toward the trailhead.

2.4   Arrive back at the trailhead.

Geocaching

Geocaching, or using a GPS receiver or other navigational technique to hide and retrieve containers, called caches, is allowed in Sweetwater, as well as in Sycamore Canyon and Mount Gower Preserve. Other parks prohibit the activity because of significant natural or cultural resources that might be disturbed.

Before you can place a cache, the county requires you to fill out a Geocache Registration Form and mail it to the appropriate person within park services. Sweetwater geocaching forms may be e-mailed to Louis.Chertkow @sdcounty.ca.gov. Call (619) 472-7572 for more information.

BonitaFest (http://bonitafest.com), held in Bonita each autumn, is an annual street fair that includes a golf tournament, in addition to the usual food and craft booths.

Less Busy, Scenic Hikes

Lake Poway provides water and recreational fishing and boating for San Diego. See Hike 12.

Part of the lure of hiking is the chance to find a little peace and quiet. If you're ready to get away from the most bustling outdoor venues and yet not desperate for complete solitude, try some of the hikes in this section. You might have moments when there is nary another sole in site. Many of these hikes will be familiar to those who regularly get out and get dirty, but we hope we've found some that you may not already have experienced.

We are always up for a walk on the beach. We've included plenty of these, and we let you know how to get to some of our favorite spots that shouldn't be overrun with tourists. For those who like to learn a little history with their hikes, we've included a number of historic destinations that vary from more challenging hikes to those that are stroller friendly. You'll also find a number of hikes that let you experience the best of San Diego's gorgeous views. Most of the hikes require just a quick drive to the trailhead and yet are isolated enough to let you return home refreshed in body and soul.

If you want to ditch the crowds and your clothes, Black's Beach is difficult to beat. This beach lies beneath the towering sandstone cliffs of Torrey Pines State Natural Reserve.

Start: The south end of Torrey Pines State Beach

Distance: 5.8 miles out and back

Approximate hiking time: 4 hours

Difficulty: Moderate due to length

Trail surface: Sand

Best season: Year-round

Other trail users: Surfers, scuba divers, snorkelers, college students, nudists, naturalists; anyone who loves a good beach

Canine compatibility: No dogs allowed

Fees and permits: Parking fee if using the Torrey Pines State Natural Reserve parking lot

Schedule: Parking available 7:00 a.m. to sunset at Torrey Pines State Natural Reserve parking lot; Gliderport parking lot open 24 hours

Maps: USGS Del Mar OEW; trail map available at www.california coastaltrail.info/hikers/hikers _main.php?DisplayAction=Display Section&CountyId=21&Section Id=398

Trail contacts: Torrey Pines State Natural Reserve, 12600 North Torrey Pines Rd., San Diego, CA 92037; (858) 755-2063; www .torreypine.org

City of San Diego; (619) 221-8899; www.sandiego.gov/park-and-recreation/parks/shoreline/ kelloggpark.shtml

Special considerations: No alcohol allowed

Other: Beach areas and trails may be inaccessible during high tide.

Finding the trailhead: Take I-5 north from San Diego. Exit onto Carmel Valley Road; turn left and drive west toward the ocean for about 1.5 miles until you reach the Pacific Coast Highway (US 101). Turn left and proceed along the beach for about 1 mile. The park entrance is a turnoff on your right, just before a large hill. Go south along Torrey Pines State Beach and park where you can. GPS: N32.9285 / W117.2596

THE HIKE

Black's Beach is one of the most interesting beaches in the state. According to city and state records, Black's Beach does not officially exist by that name. The name refers to a 2-mile stretch of coast at the intersection of Torrey Pines State Beach (managed by Torrey Pines State Natural Reserve) to the north and Torrey Pines City Beach (managed by the City of San Diego) to the south. While nudity has been illegal on the city-managed portion of the beach since 1977, it is still tolerated on the portion managed by the state. The steel buoy on the north and about 100 yards south of the Gliderport Trail marks the boundary. Tide pools can be found at Flat Rock, a distinctively large rock just below the Torrey Pines State Natural Reserve beach access trail.

Although there are no quick and easy ways to access Black's Beach, many surfers and nudists are willing to make the trek. Powerful surf breaks are created as the water travels over Scripps Canyon, an underwater canyon located just offshore. The waves here can be large and break quickly, which makes it a favorite for the aggressive crowds but dangerous for a novice surfer. People who are just learning would do better a little farther south in the calmer waters off La Jolla Shores Beach near the Scripps Pier.

Part of what creates the unique flavor of Black's Beach is its somewhat remote location. There are only four ways into the beach, all of which require some sort of

The relative difficulty in getting to Black's Beach is the chief reason the crowds are so thin.

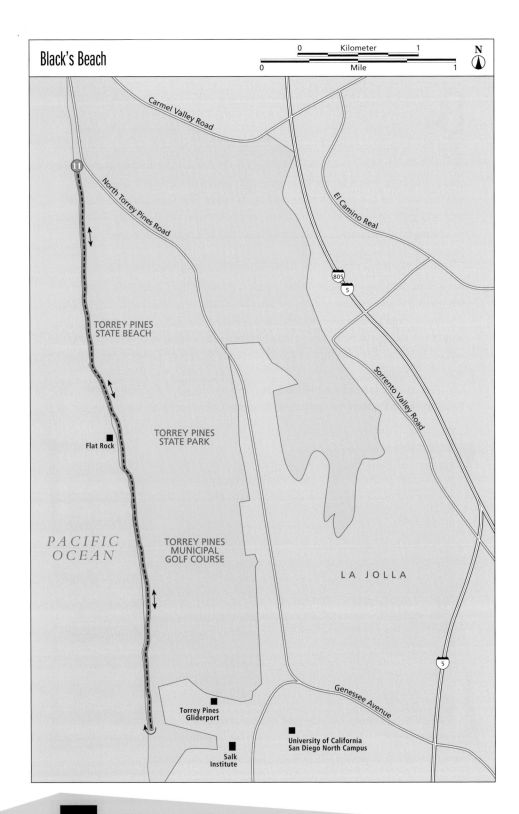

0   Kilometer   1

0   Mile   1

N

Carmel Valley Road

North Torrey Pines Road

El Camino Real

11

805

5

TORREY PINES
STATE BEACH

Sorrento Valley Road

TORREY PINES
STATE PARK

Flat Rock

PACIFIC
OCEAN

TORREY PINES
MUNICIPAL
GOLF COURSE

LA JOLLA

5

Genessee Avenue

Torrey Pines
Gliderport

University of California
San Diego North Campus

Salk
Institute

hike. The lack of direct access means that you'll never see the large crowds that frequent the adjacent Torrey Pines State Beach or La Jolla Shores. The Gliderport Trail, while popular, has a 300-foot elevation differential and is quite steep. Access from Torrey Pines State Beach to the north and La Jolla Shores Beach from the south is not possible during high tide, and the access points are a few miles away. The easiest way is probably through Salk Canyon, which features a paved road from the University of California San Diego campus to 0.5 mile south of the Gliderport Trail. This route is an obvious favorite for university students.

MILES AND DIRECTIONS

0.0   Start at the Torrey Pines State Natural Reserve parking lot and head south along the beach.

0.9   Reach Flat Rock.

1.8   Arrive at the large steel buoy that marks the beginning of the clothing-optional area.

2.9   Arrive at Torrey Pines Gliderport. Return the way you came.

5.8   Arrive back at the trailhead.

While nudity is allowed on the northern half of Black's Beach, it is certainly not required. As long as you respect the privacy of others, there is no stigma against enjoying the beach with clothes on. Nude beach etiquette is often posted at the bottom of the Gliderport Trail.

Blue Sky Ecological Reserve

Blue Sky Ecological Reserve takes you into backcountry that includes a walk by a stream that feeds into Lake Poway. With miles of trails, it is easy to spend the day here, hiking in and out of shade before enjoying a dip in the lake. This California state reserve is one of the most frequented in the system because of the variety of hiking experiences it offers, from cool forests to hot, open chaparral to lakeside walks. Kids love to fish off the small pier, while teens head to the lake for an after-school dip. It isn't unusual to see Poway High School cross-country teams practicing along the hills.

Start: Gate at the south end of the parking area
Distance: 5.2-mile lollipop
Approximate hiking time: 3 hours
Difficulty: Moderate due to length and inclines
Trail surface: Dirt path
Best season: Summer, when you can enjoy a quick dip in the lake; spring, when lupines, monkey flower, and chaparral are in bloom
Other trail users: Equestrians, teens headed to the lake to swim
Canine compatibility: Leashed (6-foot leash) dogs allowed on main trail only. (You must clean up after your pet.)

Fees and permits: No fees or permits required
Schedule: Reserve open daylight hours year-round
Maps: USGS Escondido; trail maps available online at www .blueskyreserve.org/images/blue skymap.pdf and www.dfg .ca.gov/lands/er/region5/docs/ BlueSky_BodenCanyonER.pdf
Trail contacts: Blue Sky Ecological Reserve, P.O. Box 789, Poway, CA 92074; (858) 668-4781
Special considerations: Keep your dog close to avoid encounters with rattlesnakes, ticks, and poison oak.

Finding the trailhead: Head toward Poway on I-15, exiting at Rancho Bernardo Road. Turn east and travel for about 3 miles on Rancho Bernardo Road until it becomes Espola Road. Just after you pass Old Coach Road, Espola Road curves to the right. The reserve is just past that curve on the left side of the road. If you reach Lake Poway Road, you've gone too far. The trailhead is at the end of the parking lot. GPS: N32.70821 / W117.234528

THE HIKE

With over 700 acres, Blue Sky Ecological Reserve is among the best hiking areas the California Department of Fish and Game offers to the public. Created in 1989 after the purchase of Blue Sky Ranch, this is the only reserve in San Diego County to staff a full-time naturalist. The ease of access and unique ecology make it a popular destination for locals, and the reserve is used by the City of Poway for a variety of volunteer-led themed nature hikes and campfire programs. Around 40,000 people pass through the reserve each year, and it is a favorite destination for school field trips and runners looking for a place to greet the dawn.

Blue Sky is surrounded on three sides by other permanent open spaces, allowing the trails within to be linked together with other, longer routes outside the reserve's boundaries. (Mount Woodson can be reached by heading east; staying north will net you a 5.0-mile round-trip hike to Ramona Reservoir.)The hike begins through a gate that takes you down an incline and follows a dirt road that eventually ends up at Ramona Dam. The path parallels the creek, and you can take an optional path right along the creekbed. Because poison oak and rattlesnakes are common in this area, rangers caution that dogs should always be kept on a short leash and not be allowed to wander. If your dog brushes against poison oak, the

A steep climb takes you up and over the dam to Lake Poway's glassy water.

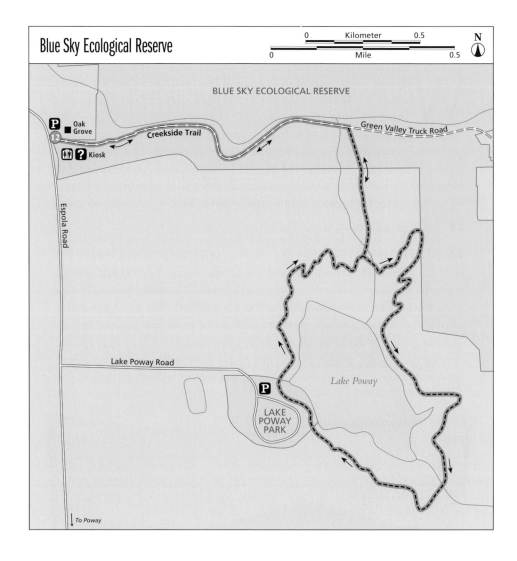

BLUE SKY ECOLOGICAL RESERVE

Green Valley Truck Road

Creekside Trail

Oak Grove

Kiosk

Espola Road

Lake Poway Road

Lake Poway

LAKE POWAY PARK

To Poway

irritating oils can be transferred to your skin when you pet him. The dense thickets of poison oak, however, do favor nature lovers with brilliant fall colors. The shady tree-lined stream is a great place to look for birds, including rails, sapsuckers, and black-shouldered kites.

The turnoff to Lake Poway takes you out of the oak groves and Blue Sky Ecological Reserve and onto land owned and managed by the City of Poway. Shortly past the campground and outdoor classroom, you will reach the fork that signals the start of the Lake Poway Loop. Either way will take you up a steep climb along a crest that affords a smashing view of both the lake and the dam. At the opposite end is Lake Poway Park, which offers ample parking and picnic areas, fishing, and small watercraft access.

The hike around the lake itself can be moderately steep and has multiple forks leading up to housing developments. Enjoy the sparkling waters and lush park before heading down the other side of Lake Poway Dam and back toward the Blue Sky Ecological Reserve parking lot.

MILES AND DIRECTIONS

0.0 Start at the trailhead at the end of the parking lot.

0.3 Turn left onto the footpath that leads to the streambed and live oak grove.

0.9 Take the path to the right and continue toward Lake Poway.

1.3 Bear left at the fork and go up and over Lake Poway Dam. (**Option:** When the road splits, the left-hand path crosses a creek and starts uphill toward the Ramona Reserve Dam. The 1.0-mile-plus hike rises 700 feet and offers a great view of Poway and San Diego County. The hot, sunny climb is best done with your most fashionable hat and plenty of drinking water.)

4.0 The trail takes you around the lake before depositing you back at the junction under the dam. Turn left to return to your starting point.

5.3 Arrive back at the parking lot.

Stick to the trail while hiking in Blue Sky Ecological Reserve—the dense forest harbors poison ivy.

Broken Hill Trail

Broken Hill Trail is considered the premier trail at Torrey Pines State Natural Reserve. Scenic overlooks and access to Torrey Pines State Beach are all part of this hike. The surroundings offer little cover, and the hike can be moderately steep at some points. The trail intersects Razor Point Trail at the beach and ties into the trail to Black's Beach. The wind-sculpted hills offer unique terrain.

Start: At the visitor center

Distance: 2.9-mile lollipop

Approximate hiking time: 3 hours

Difficulty: Moderate due to inclines

Trail surface: Concrete, dirt path, sand

Best season: Year-round

Other trail users: Runners

Canine compatibility: Leashed dogs allowed

Fees and permits: Parking fee

Schedule: Reserve open 8:00 a.m. to sunset

Maps: USGS Escondido; trail map available at www.torreypine.org/activities/hiking-trails-2.html

Trail contacts: Torrey Pines State Natural Reserve, 12600 North Torrey Pines Rd., San Diego, CA 92037; (858) 755-2063; www.torreypine.org

Special considerations: The visitor center has restrooms. Picnicking is allowed only on the beach; only water is permitted in the reserve above the beach.

Finding the trailhead: Take I-5 north from San Diego and exit onto Carmel Valley Road. Drive west (toward the ocean) for about 1.5 miles until you reach the Pacific Coast Highway (US 101). Turn left and proceed along the beach for about a mile. The reserve entrance is a turnoff on your right just before a large hill. The trailhead is to the right of the visitor center restrooms. GPS: N32.9196 / W117.2525

B roken Hill is a robust formation located between the tan sandstone cliffs along the edge of the sea. This type of cliff, commonly found along the Southern California coastline, is known as the Scripps Formation and was originally formed from the shallow seabed forty-five million years ago.

The trail offers a glimpse into the rugged nature of the area sans development. San Diego County has a semi-arid climate, and the ecosystem within this trail expresses it well. Several desert plants can be found along the trail, including yucca and prickly pear cactus. You will notice that much of the vegetation is in the form of small, shrublike plants. To survive, these plants have developed specialized features such as small or waxy leaves.

Before embarking on the trail, enjoy the visitor center, located on the east side of the parking lot. There you'll find a small museum featuring natural and cultural history. The road that you took up here continues through a barrier that marks the end of vehicle traffic. Past this point you will notice the forest thins out fairly quickly. You may also notice a good number of dead Torrey pine trees, victims of drought and bark beetle infestation. The Torrey pine tree is the rarest pine tree in the Americas, growing natively in only two places (Torrey Pines State Natural Reserve and Santa Rosa Island). More than 50 percent of the total natural population now lies within the reserve.

Broken Hill, as its name implies, is a jagged expanse of rock and cliff.

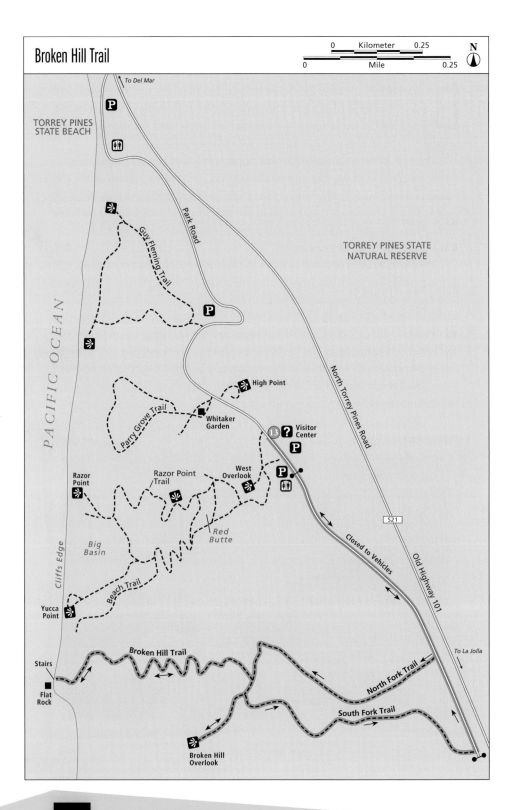

Broken Hill Trail

0 Kilometer 0.25
0 Mile 0.25

N

TORREY PINES STATE BEACH

To Del Mar

P

Guy Fleming Trail

Park Road

TORREY PINES STATE NATURAL RESERVE

PACIFIC OCEAN

P

High Point

Parry Grove Trail

Whitaker Garden

13 ? Visitor Center

P

North Torrey Pines Road

Razor Point

Razor Point Trail

West Overlook

P

Big Basin

Red Butte

S21

Closed to Vehicles

Old Highway 101

Cliffs Edge

Beach Trail

Yucca Point

Stairs

Flat Rock

Broken Hill Trail

North Fork Trail

To La Jolla

South Fork Trail

Broken Hill Overlook

As you make your way down the trail, you'll spot the beach right around the time you encounter a series of mild switchbacks. At the bottom you will find a set of stairs that leads down to Torrey Pines State Beach. You can easily walk north, back to the park entrance, or south as far as Black's Beach or La Jolla. Flat Rock is a formation located just south of the stairs, and you can find tide pools there during the day.

MILES AND DIRECTIONS

0.0 Start from the visitor center; continue on the road past the vehicle barrier.

0.4 Turn right onto the North Fork Trail and head toward the ocean. The path is well marked.

0.7 Reach a junction with the South Fork Trail and a short path to Broken Hill. For now, keep right.

1.2 Take the stairs down to Torrey Pines State Beach. Flat Rock, just down the beach, contains tide pools. (**Options:** From here you can either walk up the beach back toward the park entrance or down to Black's Beach. This hike can be connected with the Razor Point Trail via the Beach Trail.) When you're done exploring, climb the stairs back up to the trail.

1.6 Arrive back at the junction with the South Fork Trail and the path to Broken Hill. Turn right to access the Broken Hill viewpoint.

1.7 Reach the viewpoint. From here you can see Broken Hill as well as Torrey Pines Golf Course to your left. Backtrack to the junction; take the South Fork Trail to your immediate right.

2.3 Reconnect with the road. Turn left to continue back the way you came.

2.9 Arrive back at the visitor center.

Cowles Mountain

Panoramic views of San Diego County from its foothills to its blue shoreline lure hikers to this inland peak. Three trails access this extremely popular viewpoint, so if quiet solitude is your goal, pick another hike. But you can't say you've hiked San Diego County if you haven't hiked Cowles Mountain.

Start: West side of the road, just north of the park entrance

Distance: 4.4 miles out and back

Approximate hiking time: 3 hours

Difficulty: Difficult due to elevation gain

Trail surface: Dirt with some railroad ties and steps to prevent erosion and facilitate climbing

Best season: Winter and spring, when the rains make the area lush

Other trail users: Mountain bikers, athletes in training

Canine compatibility: Leashed dogs allowed

Fees and permits: No fees or permits required

Schedule: Sunrise to sunset; visitor center open daily 9:00 a.m. to 5:00 p.m.; closed Thanksgiving Day, Christmas Day, and New Year's Day

Maps: USGS La Mesa; trail maps available at www.mtrp.org/trail_map.asp and www.sandiego.gov/park-and-recreation/pdf/missiontrailstrailmap.pdf

Trail contacts: Mission Trails Regional Park, 1 Father Junipero Serra Trail, San Diego, CA 92119; (619) 668-3275 or (619) 668-3281; www.mtrp.org

Special considerations: Don't miss the visitor and interpretive center with its views of the gorge.

Finding the trailhead: From I-5, I-805, CA-163, or I-15, take CA 52 east, heading toward Santee. Turn right (west) onto Mission Gorge Road and proceed 0.4 mile before turning left (south) onto Mesa Road. The trailhead is approximately a half mile down the road on the right side, just beyond Big Rock Park and Prospect Avenue. GPS: N32.829838 / W117.017889

THE HIKE

One of the best inland hikes in San Diego, Cowles Mountain offers incredible panoramic views from its 1,592-foot peak, the highest point within the San Diego city limits. From this perch, on a clear day you can see the ocean, with the Coronado Islands rising from the mist, and the city skyline, with Mexico as a backdrop. The Santee Lakes lie to the north like a breath of life. Most interestingly, you can see the way the watershed pours from the hills to the ocean, as fingers of water flow from Mission Valley to the sea.

Most of the area consists of low-growing "hard" chaparral tucked into rocky terrain. The dense shrubbery is almost impossible to move through, so staying on the path is both a necessity and the right thing to do to preserve this heavily used preserve.

Lake Murray sparkles at the foot of Cowles Mountain.

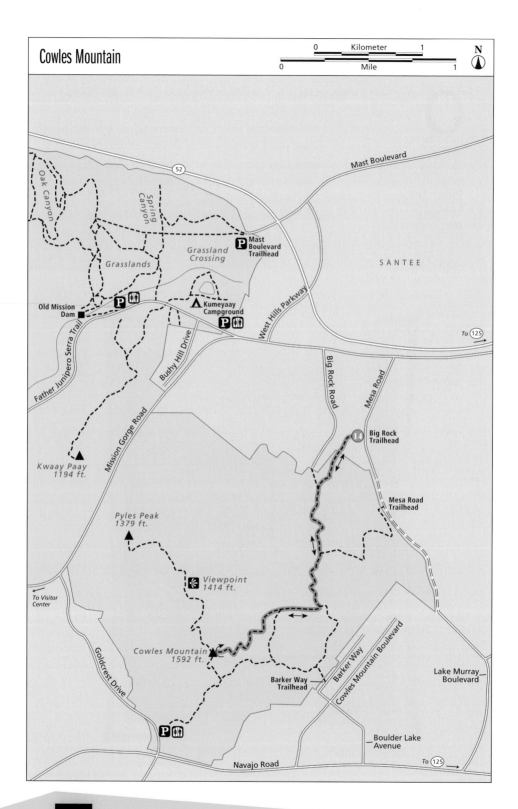

Cowles Mountain

This side of the popular summit is the greenest, since it faces north and gets the most moisture. That means that scrub oak, redberry, mission manzanita, and chamise are thicker and more abundant than on other trails up the mountain. Minty black sage fills with balls of purple flowers that are a favorite of honeybees. In February the purple and blue blooms of wild California lilac remind Westerners of the eastern lilac (no relation). Look for swallowtail butterflies amidst the leaves.

In April and May, small, orange, cuplike California poppies take over. From April through June, baby blue eyes stand 2 to 3 feet tall and produce bell-shaped flowers. Both the poppy and baby blue eyes need a fire the year before to produce their best blooms.

Lizards, small rodents, coyotes, skunks, and numerous snakes also take advantage of the lush northern slope. You also will most likely see many kinds of butterflies, including fritillaries and sulphurs.

The hike begins through bright-green grassy landscape and continues sharply uphill after meandering alongside Big Rock Creek. This is the least-traveled path to the summit. Once scarred by off-road vehicles and erosion, the mountainside has healed nicely. Continue up the steep grade, taking time to smell the chaparral. Park personnel have added railroad ties and steps to ease the runoff after a rain and help prevent further erosion. Continue climbing, enjoying the varying views provided by the switchbacks, until you reach the summit.

Whatever the weather, the view from the stop is spectacular. Morning mists make the coastal area appear to float in the sea. Crystal-clear days may let you glimpse Catalina Island. Rain offers the chance of a waterfall at the base of the mountain near the Mesa side of Big Rock Park. Sunrises and sunsets enrich the blues, greens, and browns of the valley and beyond. Pick your pleasure—as long as it isn't solitude—before heading back down the mountain.

MILES AND DIRECTIONS

0.0 Start at the trailhead on the west side of Mesa Road, just past the park entrance.

0.8 Continue up the mountain when the trail merges with a trail to the Mesa Road trailhead.

1.3 The trail merges with Barker Way Service Road.

2.2 Reach the summit; relax before returning the way you came.

4.4 Arrive back at the trailhead.

Dog Beach Mudflat

The muddy delta at the mouth of the San Diego River is home to an endangered California least tern nesting area and countless other waterbirds. This popular destination is one of the best places to frolic with your favorite dog. You'll also find anglers, crabbers, and beachcombers. The trails are worn footpaths that change with the water levels and sandy beaches that appear and disappear with the tide.

Start: At the parking lot on the west end of Robb Field

Distance: 1.0-mile out and back

Approximate hiking time: 1 hour

Difficulty: Easy

Trail surface: Wet and dry sand

Best season: Summer, when least terns are breeding

Other trail users: Crabbers, anglers, people with dogs

Canine compatibility: Dogs free to frolic off-leash. (You must clean up after your pet.)

Fees and permits: No fees or permits required

Schedule: Open 24 hours

Maps: USGS La Jolla OEW

Trail contacts: San Diego County Beaches, Dog Beach (at Ocean Beach); (619) 221-8899
   County Administration Center, 1600 Pacific Hwy., San Diego, CA 92101; (619) 221-8899

Special considerations: Do not allow your dog to disturb the terns.

Finding the trailhead: Take I-8 westbound toward the beaches and exit onto Sunset Cliffs Boulevard. Take the first right onto West Point Loma Boulevard. Turn right into the first access street past Bacon Street and into a dirt parking area. Climb the berm and take the path headed toward the ocean. Then take the first path down into the delta. GPS: N32.754848 / W117.246314

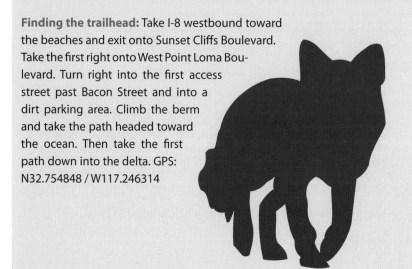

THE HIKE

This unscripted hike begins at a hidden parking lot that lets you climb onto the trail alongside the San Diego River. Continue toward the sea, taking the first trail down into the delta. There are some established paths to the beach or onto the delta, but I suspect that they aren't reliable. Dogs frolic in the waves, in the sand, and with one another—after all, this is part of Dog Beach.

In the center of the mudflat is a California least tern breeding sanctuary surrounded by an open wire fence. The terns are fun to watch, and if you walk by the breeding ground, you can hear their computer chip–like chirps. The 10-inch-long white birds with black heads, pale gray wings, and bright-yellow bills and feet are the only tern subspecies in California. They thrive on coastal estuaries, where they dive for small fish including smelt, anchovies, and silversides. Spend a few minutes watching for their unique swooping flight pattern. Your eyes can follow a tern as it hovers in the air looking for prey, dive-bombs down into the water, and hopefully comes back up with dinner. We watched one tern attempt to catch his supper over and over, continually surfacing with an empty bill. It was hard not to want to go to the bait shop and throw him a bone, so to speak. Another tern (another day) appeared to have caught a fish, but the fish stayed in its mouth for well over fifteen minutes, making us suspect that he had speared rather than caught it. Perhaps a helpful friend eventually would help get the fish off his bill and into his mouth.

Ocean Beach Pier extends far into the Pacific Ocean.

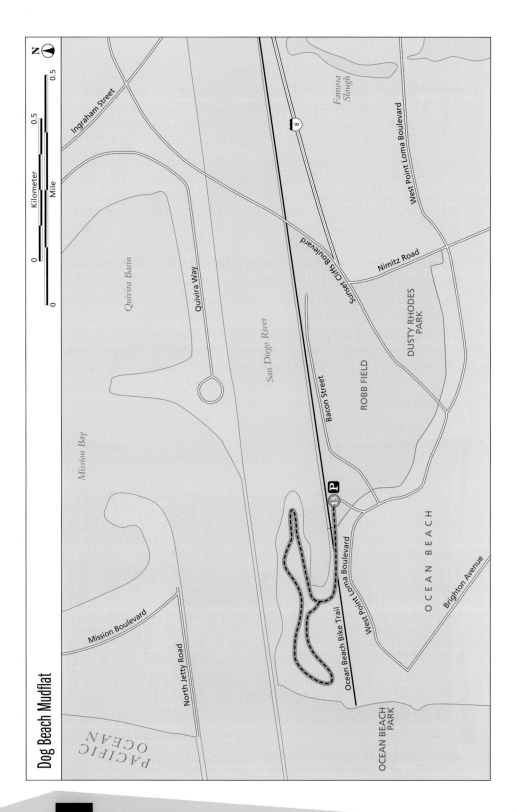

Dog Beach Mudflat

Least terns once lived all along the central and southern California coast down through the coast of Mexico. Today most breeding pairs reside within Southern California. The terns live in colonies of thirty to fifty mating pairs. They nest in close proximity and leave the nesting area to gather on nearby mudflats and return in clusters. Terns lay their eggs in the sand or gravel in shallow depressions near water.

The colony congregates from April through September, with nesting commencing in mid-May. Nesting pairs produce two or three eggs, which are incubated by both adults. In a little less than a month, the hatchlings emerge and are cared for by both parents until they are old enough to fly, at about three weeks. After one to two weeks of practice, the fledglings leave the nest but still rely on their parents to help provide dinner for a couple of additional weeks.

This significant breeding and care time is disrupted if the birds can't find conducive areas for their colony to set down. Because terns prefer to nest close to the shoreline, beachside development impacts their nesting choices. When they are forced to nest too closely together, they are easier to pick off by a host of predators, including American kestrels, burrowing owls, crows, cats, and foxes.

Wander around the dunes and mudflat, trying to keep your feet from getting too muddy. You'll get a chance to interact with kids, anglers, happy dogs, and plenty of birds in addition to the terns, including ibis, pelicans, and finches. When you're done exploring, head back to the path that led you down.

Giant wet dog paws glimmer in the rain, marking the entrance to Dog Beach.

15

A Hiker's Call to Act

For decades the coast along the southernmost border of San Diego has suffered episodes of pollution from sewage runoff so severe that it shut the beaches down. And for decades plans have been in the works to resolve the issue. As recently as October 2010, stormwater pollution closed beaches for seventy-two hours throughout San Diego County.

The Tijuana Slough had additional warnings. Sewage-laden runoff poured into the ocean from the Tijuana River. Northward-moving currents carried the contaminated water up along the coast of Imperial Beach, perhaps as far north as Silver Strand State Park.

While San Diegans love rain, they don't love the pollution and bacteria that the rainwater washes into the sea. Bacteria levels can rise quickly offshore and within the bays near storm drains and the natural tributaries that flow to the ocean. The runoff picks up bacteria from animal waste, decomposing vegetation, soil, and debris from hard surface areas. The more hardscaping the county adds, the more accumulated bacteria washes from pavement into the sea whenever it rains.

Unfortunately, cement and other nonpermeable hard surfaces are becoming more common within San Diego County's infrastructure as it attempts to deal with the heavy foot traffic created by three million residents and nearly fifteen million visitors each year. Hard surfaces not only keep water from soaking into the ground and recharging aquifers but also exacerbate erosion on the remaining areas where water flows.

As San Diego continues to expand even as it fights to reenergize its native ecosystems and add trails into the newly revitalized wilds, the city should think about letting nature do its thing. Options include joining the green roof movement and expanding native vegetation within key watershed areas. Not only is it healthier for surfers, swimmers, and coastal hikers, it's also healthier for the planet.

It is the rare hiker who hikes simply to get his or her cardio in. Who better than hikers to educate the community and those in charge of creating hiking paths about good landscape design and how it impacts the rest of the environment? That is a challenge hikers could spearhead for the next hundred years.

Guy Fleming Trail

The variety and peace of Torrey Pines State Natural Reserve attract a faithful follow-ing who breathe in the scent of eucalyptus while enjoying the clifftop breezes above the sea. This trail is named for Guy Fleming, one of the most influential pioneers in the San Diego park system. Fleming was the Lorax for the Torrey Pines and may have inspired Dr. Seuss, who lived just down the road and whose main character in his book The Lorax *famously tries to protect a doomed forest of Truffula Trees.*

Start: Trailhead just uphill from the parking area
Distance: 0.7-mile lollipop
Approximate hiking time: 30 minutes
Difficulty: Easy
Trail surface: Dirt path
Best season: Year-round
Other trail users: Runners
Canine compatibility: Leashed dogs allowed
Fees and permits: Parking fee
Schedule: 8:00 a.m. to sunset

Maps: USGS Escondido; trail map available online at www .torreypine.org/activities/ hiking-trails-2.html
Trail contacts: Torrey Pines State Natural Reserve, 12600 North Torrey Pines Rd., San Diego, CA 92037; (858) 755-2063; www .torreypine.org
Special considerations: The visi-tor center has restrooms. Picnick-ing is allowed only on the beach; only water is permitted in the reserve above the beach.

Finding the trailhead: Take I-5 north from San Diego. Exit onto Carmel Valley Road; turn left and drive west toward the ocean for about 1.5 miles until you reach the Pacific Coast Highway (US 101). Turn left onto the Coast Highway and proceed along the beach for about 1 mile. The park entrance is a turnoff on your right just before a large hill. Take the road into the park. After about 0.5 mile, reach a small parking area on the right side of the road. Just uphill from the parking lot is the marked trailhead for the Guy Fleming Trail. GPS: N32.9196 / W117.2525

THE HIKE

Tucked into the northern corner of Torrey Pines State Natural Reserve, the Guy Fleming Trail gets its name from the reserve's original custodian and naturalist.

Although not officially named until 1850 by Dr. Charles Parry, the Torrey pine was identified as a rare tree as far back as the 1500s by Spanish explorers, who called them *soledad* or solitary pines. These unique pines were thought to grow only on the narrow strip of land that is now the reserve until 1888, when another grove was discovered 175 miles away on Santa Rosa Island.

In 1921 the land that would become Torrey Pines Reserve was owned partially by the City of San Diego and partially by early San Diego philanthropist Miss Ellen Scripps, who had purchased the land specifically to protect the Torrey pine. That year, Miss Scripps and the city hired Guy Fleming to be the area's custodian. When Fleming married in 1927, he built a house on Miss Scripps's land out of material he salvaged from the burned remains of San Diego's first natural history museum. The house is now part of the Scripps Institution of Oceanography.

In 1932, after helping the newly created state park system acquire a number of parklands, Fleming was hired as district superintendent over all state parks in Southern California. Even after retiring in 1948, Fleming kept working to protect this special area. Along with neighbors and a few friends, Fleming founded the

A truly stunning view is the reward for those willing to take the often-overlooked Guy Fleming Trail.

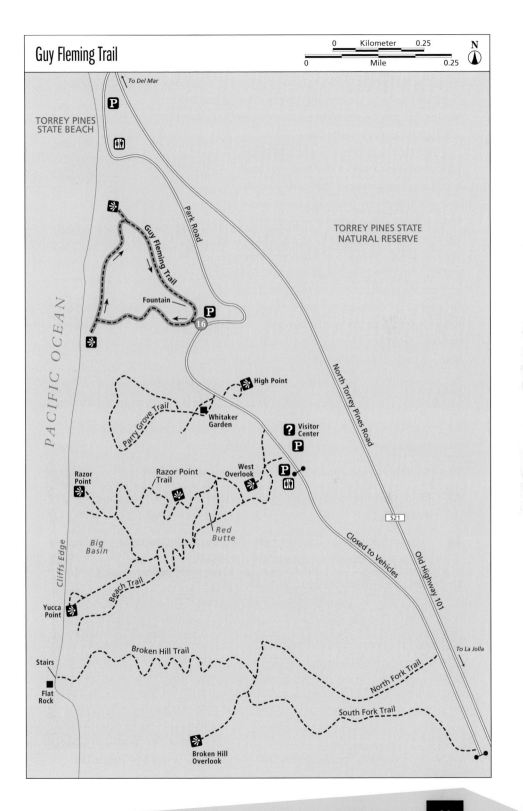

Guy Fleming Trail

0 ...... Kilometer 0.25

0 ...... Mile 0.25

N

TORREY PINES STATE BEACH

To Del Mar

Park Road

Guy Fleming Trail

Fountain

16

TORREY PINES STATE NATURAL RESERVE

PACIFIC OCEAN

High Point

Parry Grove Trail

Whitaker Garden

Visitor Center

Razor Point

Razor Point Trail

West Overlook

North Torrey Pines Road

Red Butte

S21

Big Basin

Cliffs Edge

Beach Trail

Closed to Vehicles

Old Highway 101

Yucca Point

Broken Hill Trail

North Fork Trail

To La Jolla

Stairs

Flat Rock

South Fork Trail

Broken Hill Overlook

Torrey Pines Association in 1950 with the intent of bringing what was then Torrey Pines City Park under the authority and greater protection of the state park system. The state took over the park officially in 1959. Having lived to see his life's work accomplished, Fleming died on May 15, 1960, at the age of seventy-five.

Stomped out over the years by thousands of pairs of shoes, the trail was well established long before the park planners ever got there. Guy Fleming himself loved to bring visitors down the shady path and to the stunning overlooks. The city of La Jolla can be seen in its full glory at the southern viewpoint, trailing along the cove's wide embrace. Trekking up from the south end, you're met with a spectacular view of Los Peñasquitos Marsh and a long line of sand as Torrey Pines State Beach stretches to the north. The outlook features a small bench that puts you right on the edge of the stunning vista that seems to attract young and old lovers alike—it begs to be shared with someone you love.

MILES AND DIRECTIONS

0.0   Start at the parking lot just uphill from the main entrance. Continue up the road a short ways to reach the marked trailhead.

0.1   Arrive at the loop junction. Smell the forest and head left.

0.4   Reach the viewpoint that overlooks Torrey Pines State Beach and the salt marsh.

0.6   Take a drink from the fountain before hitting the loop junction once again; turn left and retrace your steps to the trailhead.

0.7   Arrive back at the trailhead and parking lot.

Ocean Beach Pier

Ocean Beach is a unique example of Southern California culture. With the exception of a Starbucks, almost no national franchises have made their way into this community. The vast majority of businesses are locally owned mom-and-pop-type establishments, giving Ocean Beach distinct personality and charm.

Start: Right side of parking lot on Voltaire Street

Distance: 1.2 miles out and back

Approximate hiking time: 1 hour

Difficulty: Easy

Trail surface: Wet and dry sand

Best season: Year-round

Other trail users: People with dogs, people fishing, families

Canine compatibility: Leashed dogs allowed

Fees and permits: No fees or permits required

Schedule: Beach open 24 hours

Maps: USGS La Jolla OEW

Trail contacts: San Diego County Beaches, Dog Beach (at Ocean Beach); (619) 221-8899

County Administration Center, 1600 Pacific Hwy., San Diego, CA 92101; (619) 221-8899

Special considerations: Dogs are allowed off-leash north of the Voltaire Street parking lot, on-leash down to the pier.

Finding the trailhead: Take I-8 westbound toward the beaches and exit onto Sunset Cliffs Boulevard. Make the first right onto West Point Loma Boulevard and travel less than 1 mile before turning right onto Voltaire Street and then into the parking lot. The pier is to your left as you face the ocean. GPS: N32.754333 / W117.251619

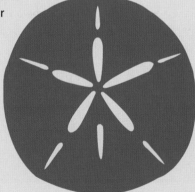

Dog Beach is one of San Diego's great under-recognized gems. Located in Ocean Beach, the area north of the Voltaire Street parking lot is designated as San Diego County's first leash-free coastal zone. Informally called Dog Beach, this friendly and open stretch of sand is absolutely one of the best places in the country to bring your dog.

Begin your hike after frolicking with your best friend on the northern end of Ocean Beach for leash-free doggie fun, then leash up to head toward the pier, noting the fantastic selection of local cuisine along Abbot Street.

The Ocean Beach Municipal Pier is a destination in itself. Stretching 1,971 feet out into the Pacific Ocean, it's the longest concrete pier in San Diego County. No permit is required to fish off the pier, making it an extraordinary place for families to kill an afternoon. A bait shop and restaurant float at the end of the pier, offering bait and equipment to help you get your fishing fix. It also offers spectacular views from the end of the pier, along with people and pelican watching.

The pier is open twenty-four hours a day. Although you may occasionally hear reports that the pier is unsafe at night, crime hasn't been much of a problem since police started frequent bicycle patrols in the late '90s. You can come to Ocean Beach Pier at any time of day (or night) without worry of hooligan harassment. After enjoying the pier, return the way you came.

Reaching into the Pacific, Ocean Beach Pier makes for a pleasant maritime walk—at any time of day.

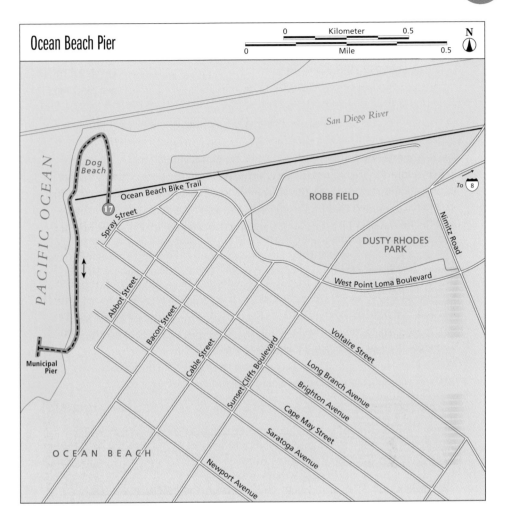

17

Ocean Beach Pier

MILES AND DIRECTIONS

0.0   Start at the Voltaire Street parking lot and take a minute to explore Dog Beach before heading south along the coast.

0.1   Pass some volleyball nets on the beach. The locals are usually happy to let a new person join in.

0.3   To your left is a grassy area with a picnic table. Enjoy a sandwich and such.

0.5   Abbot Street is on your left. (**Option:** Follow Abbot Street inland and shop at Ocean Beach's small and interesting stores.)

0.6 Arrive at Ocean Beach Municipal Pier. Fish, or merely enjoy the sights. Retrace your steps.

1.2 Arrive back at the Voltaire Street parking lot.

A Pooch-Friendly California

Fortunately for canines and their human companions, California has become increasingly dog friendly. Many San Diego beaches are now welcoming to pet owners, and some are leash-free. Fiesta Island, located in Mission Bay, is one such area. Dogs can explore the entire island leash-free, and the calm water is perfect for a pet that loves to swim. As watercraft frequent the surrounding waters, use caution when selecting a place for you and your dog to take a dip.

A bit north, in Del Mar, dogs are allowed along the entire 2-mile stretch of beach for most of the year. For a dog owner, Del Mar Beach can be broken down into three areas, generally called North Beach (29th Street to Solana Beach), Main Beach (northern half of Powerhouse Park to 29th Street), and South Beach (southern half of Powerhouse Park to Torrey Pines Beach). North Beach is also known as Dog Beach, because dogs can enjoy the beach sans leash, except between June 15 and Labor Day. Dogs are allowed on Main Beach with leashes after Labor Day but not after June 15. South Beach is a little less complicated, with dogs being allowed on-leash year-round.

Beacon's Beach to Moonlight Beach

This hike between South Carlsbad and Moonlight State Beaches offers towering cliffs—sometimes into remote coves—and broad stretches of white sand that blend into the distinctive shoreline that defines the Southern California coast. Set mostly in front of private homes, the view to the west offers spectacular beach and sea views, while the view to the east lets you see how the other half (or .01 percent) lives.

Start: The public parking area at Beacon's Beach; from there, head down the switchback path to the beach

Distance: 1.2 miles point to point

Approximate hiking time: A leisurely 2 hours

Difficulty: Easy during low tide; some areas impassable during high tide

Trail surface: Sand

Best season: Summer

Other trail users: Beachcombers, surfers, occasional sea lions

Canine compatibility: No dogs allowed

Fees and permits: No fees or permits required

Schedule: Beach use 4:00 a.m. to 2 a.m.; beach parking 5:00 a.m. to 10 p.m.

Maps: USGS Encinitas; trail map available online at www .californiacoastaltrail.info/hikers/ hikers_main.php?DisplayAction =DisplaySection&CountyId=20& SectionId=421

Trail contacts: Beacon's Beach, 948 Neptune Ave., Encinitas, CA 92024; (760) 633-2740

Moonlight State Beach, 400 B St., Encinitas, CA 92024

Other: Before heading out, check the tide tables at http://wavecast .com/tide/.

Finding the trailhead: Take exit 43 off I-5 onto Leucadia Boulevard west. Follow Leucadia until you reach Neptune Avenue, the street that parallels the coast. Park at the public parking area at Neptune Avenue and West Leucadia Boulevard, and head down the switchback path to the beach. GPS: N33.064787 / W117.3044

This section of the California coast is dotted with quaint, picturesque beach towns with those ubiquitous luxury beachfront homes but also street after street of pretty cottages bursting with flowers. The streets feature skateboard- and surfer-passing signs instead of wild animal warnings. California-blond surfers (men and women) regularly stroll by, surfboard confidently slung under their arms. Restaurants are plentiful and unique. If they are part of a small chain, it is likely the mother restaurant started in one of these quaint towns.

Encinitas actually consists of five distinct communities that have incorporated as the City of Encinitas, which may be confusing when you are trying to find something and it is listed under multiple names. The section of town that lines the Pacific Coast Highway (US 101) is considered "Historic Encinitas." The section that is distinguished by colorful hillside homes overlooking the sea is "Cardiff-by-the-Sea." "Leucadia" is filled with giant eucalyptus trees that line its section of the Coast Highway. Two inland communities complete the "City."

Each year in downtown Encinitas, the Annual Fall Festival, once known as the Poinsettia Festival for the area's main agricultural export, celebrates the changing of the seasons.

A lone surfer approaches the waves.

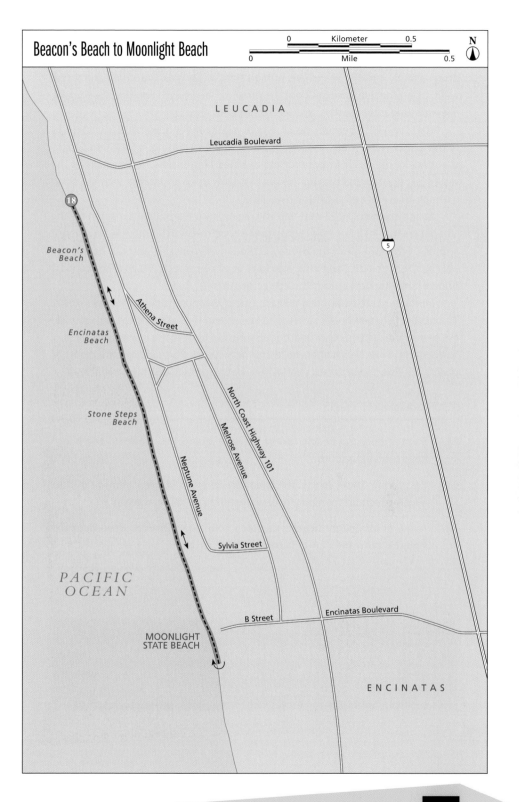

Beacon's Beach to Moonlight Beach

0 Kilometer 0.5
0 Mile 0.5

N

LEUCADIA

Leucadia Boulevard

18

Beacon's
Beach

Athena Street

Encinatas
Beach

North Coast Highway 101

Melrose Avenue

Stone Steps
Beach

Neptune Avenue

Sylvia Street

PACIFIC
OCEAN

B Street

Encinatas Boulevard

MOONLIGHT
STATE BEACH

ENCINATAS

18

This hike begins in Leucadia and runs down to Encinitas. The cliffs often drop down directly into the sea where, at high tide, waves crash into the natural seawalls. When the tide goes back out, a narrow, isolated beach emerges that quickly fills with sunbathers, surfers, and sand sculptures.

Start the hike at Beacon's Beach, where you meander downhill on switchbacks to the beach. Head south, watching some of the best surfing in Southern California at one of the locals' favorite surfing beaches. (Top surfers, however, prefer the waves just north of the beach.) The beach is fairly open and stable, with hills filled with shrubbery as well as clifftop dwellings.

At approximately 0.25 mile you will reach Stone Steps Beach, named for the steep stairs that lead from the clifftop to the beach below. This may be the quietest section of the hike, since the beach becomes even narrower and can be impassable during high tide. Make sure you don't become trapped within this section by underestimating how quickly the tide comes in.

Continue south to Moonlight Beach, one of the most popular beaches in town. The crescent-shaped beach suddenly expands and is usually packed with picnickers, teens, families, and other beachgoers who like to be in the center of the action. This section of the beach offers volleyball nets, fire pits, a snack bar, and plenty of parking. Get someone to pick you up here, or turn around and hike on back.

MILES AND DIRECTIONS

0.0 Start at Beacon's Beach, taking the switchback trail down to the beach before heading south.

0.25 Pass Stone Steps Beach. This area can be inaccessible during high tide. (**Option:** Jog up the stairs to view the noted mural on the wall.)

1.2 Arrive at Moonlight Beach and catch your ride. (**Option:** Head back the way you came for a 2.4-mile round-trip.)

In September each year, Moonlight State Beach hosts the Wavecrest Woodie Meet, the largest rally of wooden-bodied vehicles in the world.

Los Peñasquitos Canyon Preserve

Although popular, and dead center in the middle of a populated urban area, Los Peñasquitos always seems a little remote. The hike begins at the newest trailhead and ends at a remote waterfall, with spectacular rock formations and forested glens in between. Multiple intersecting multiuse trails all culminate at the path to the waterfall or to Rancho de los Peñasquitos, a historic ranch house that serves as the preserve's visitor center.

Start: The first parking lot at Camino Ruiz Community Park

Distance: 4.8 miles out and back

Approximate hiking time: 2 to 3 hours

Difficulty: Moderate due to the steepness of the first part

Trail surface: Dirt path

Best season: Year-round

Other trail users: Cyclists on designated trails

Canine compatibility: Leashed dogs allowed

Fees and permits: No fees or permits required

Schedule: Parking lots open 8:00 a.m. to sunset

Maps: USGS Del Mar; trail map available at www.co.san-diego .ca.us/reusable_components/ images/parks/doc/Trails_Los_ Penasquitos.pdf

Trail contacts: Los Peñasquitos Canyon Preserve, 12020 Black Mountain Rd., San Diego, CA 92129; (858) 484-7504; www .co.san-diego.ca.us/parks/open space/penasquitos.html

Special considerations: No glass containers, littering, or loud noises allowed in the preserve

Other: Watch for rattlesnakes, mountain lions, and rugged terrain.

Finding the trailhead: From I-15 take the Mercy Road exit and head west for 1.4 miles. Turn right onto Black Mountain Road and then left at the first light. Follow the entry road to the Ranch House parking area to stop at the visitor center. From the visitor center, return to Black Mountain Road and head right (south). Turn right onto Capricorn Way, winding your way through a residential neighborhood. Turn right onto Camino Ruiz, which ends at Camino Ruiz Community Park. The trailhead is across the street from the first parking area. Cross the street, look for an opening in the fence, and follow the path leading to the trail kiosk. GPS: N32.933318 / W117.145991

Los Peñasquitos Canyon Preserve

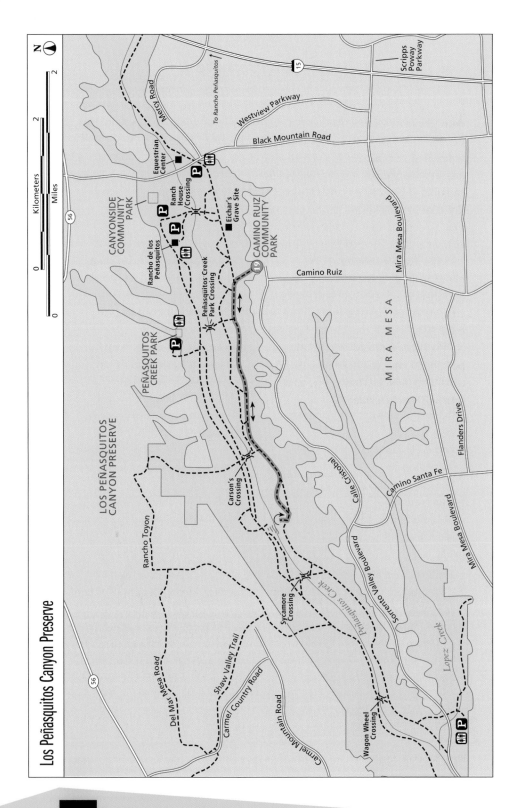

Less Busy, Scenic Hikes

THE HIKE

Los Peñasquitos Canyon is another example of a great outdoor recreation area located within an urban space. At 3,700 acres, there are few places that have as much to offer in such an accessible place. There are more than 10 miles of trails in Peñasquitos Canyon, and most are open to equestrian and bicycle use. There is a staging area at the eastern end of the park where you can unload your horses and park your trailer (for a fee). With the exception of a few places that ascend the canyon walls, horses are allowed on all trails and should be yielded to by bikers and hikers.

The canyon bottom is mostly even, with some hills. Small side paths take you along Peñasquitos Creek, and there are five bridges along the length of the trail for crossing to the north side if you wish. On the eastern end of the beginning of both the northern and southern main trails lies the historic Rancho de los Peñasquitos. The ranch house was built in 1823 on the first land grant in San Diego County and later expanded in 1862. The historic adobe structure is open to visitors, and tours are offered.

Water flows from pond to pond, creating a series of waterfalls in Los Peñasquitos Canyon Preserve.

When starting from Camino Ruiz Park, you'll find the newly created trail down the canyon to be steep and narrow, with little visibility as it winds through the shrubs. At a little over 0.5 mile, the trail doesn't last long (unless you're heading up) before reaching the forgiving canyon bottom. Although the trail is open to bike use, the slim path is a very difficult and dangerous ride for anyone who isn't an experienced mountain biker.

The canyon floor is relatively wide, and you'll spend most of the hike strolling among trees as you make your way downstream. The end of the hike rewards you with beautiful waterfalls cascading over granite boulders. The creek has carved intricate designs into the stone over the years, forming cuts reminiscent of the slot canyons found farther west. This is a great place to take pictures, but be careful—the smooth stone doesn't offer much traction.

MILES AND DIRECTIONS

0.0 Start at Camino Ruiz Community Park. The trailhead is on the left shortly after you enter the park, across the road from the first set of picnic tables. The first part of the trail takes you to the canyon bottom and is steep and narrow, with little visibility.

0.6 The path bottoms out as you reach the canyon floor. Here you meet up with the main southern river trail. Proceed left and follow the trail west.

2.3 Shortly after the 3.0-mile marker, begin walking up a large hill. You will find hitching posts and a bike rack at the crest. Take either the stairs to the right for an easy trek down to the waterfall or the path to the left for a bit of scrambling.

2.4 Arrive at the river and enjoy the series of waterfalls. Return the way you came.

4.8 Arrive back at the trailhead. Enjoy the swings at Camino Ruiz Park as you rest from the uphill climb before heading out.

Old Presidio Historic Hike

This great hike around the edge of historic Presidio Park provides a tour of the park and insight into San Diego's origins. The hike through one of the city's first and still-premier manicured gardens takes you though historic Indian burial grounds, up past the presidio, through a calming eucalyptus grove, and past a number of historical plaques. This is where the first Europeans settled and claimed San Diego as their own.

Start: At the corner of Mason and Jackson Streets

Distance: 0.8 mile out and back

Approximate hiking time: 30 minutes

Difficulty: Moderate due to the steep incline

Trail surface: Dirt path, sidewalk

Best season: Year-round

Other trail users: People with dogs, runners

Canine compatibility: Leashed dogs allowed

Fees and permits: No fees or permits required

Schedule: Open 24 hours

Maps: USGS La Jolla; trail map available online at www.sandiego .gov/park-and-recreation/pdf/ ppmap.pdf

Trail contacts: Balboa Park Administration Building, 2125 Park Blvd., San Diego, CA 92154; (619) 235-1169

Finding the trailhead: Head west on I-8 past Hotel Circle South. Exit onto Taylor Street and continue west. You will immediately see Presidio Park directly to your left. Continue on Taylor Street as it bends left before making a quick left onto Presidio Drive. Head right at the T intersection onto Jackson Street and continue for 1 block until you intersect Mason Street. Park on Mason Street. The trailhead is immediately across the road. GPS: N32.759886 / W117.192982

THE HIKE

ittle is left of the original presidio the Spanish founded in 1769, but its legacy is San Diego. When the Spanish missionaries and accompanying soldiers first arrived, the only people living in the area were the Kumeyaay. Initial attempts to convert the Kumeyaay to Christianity were largely unsuccessful, and there was an uprising only a month after the mission was established. In 1774 the padres decided to build and move to a new mission a few miles east in modern-day Mission Valley. The new mission was called Mission San Diego de Alcala.

For the first few decades the presidio population stayed almost entirely within the safety of the presidio walls, farming along the valley within the comfort of cannon range. It all began to change in 1822, when Mexico won independence from Spain. While under Spanish rule, the presidio populace all farmed and lived off of common land, while the best tracks were held by the Church.

Donated by the Ellen Browning Scripps Foundation, *The Indian* is a tribute to the Native Americans who populated early San Diego.

Mexico did two things that vastly changed the social and political landscape: First, in 1833 it secularized the California missions. Second, all land, including the Church's, was divided up and given over to private use. This brief era of the "Californios" created enormous wealth for the recipients of that land before the United States took control after the Mexican-American War. These two factors were devastating to the mission, the population of which dwindled to 500 by 1842 and down to 100 within the next two years. In 1845 Pio Pico, governor of Alta California, sold Mission San Diego de Alcala to finance the impending war with the United States.

The presidio ceased to be a political epicenter (along with Old Town) when it burned down in 1872 along with most of the business area. Power was permanently shifted to newer settlements in the south. Today little remains of the old presidio. Besides the intermittent archaeological dig and the Padre Cross, built in 1913 out of tiles from the ruins, there is little to make you believe that a vast fortress once stood here.

Presidio Park is huge compared with a typical city park and offers many trails as well as its history to explore. It was designed primarily by Kate Sessions and George Marston as an urban garden, with over 20,000 plantings installed in 1929. During the Depression, the Works Progress Administration dug ditches, graded roads, and installed additional infrastructure that still exists today. Located on the hilltop where the presidio once stood, the Junipero Serra Museum was built in 1929 to resemble an early Spanish mission. Inside you can gain an even greater depth of knowledge about early San Diego. The museum is fun and interesting, certainly worth the modest price of admission.

The hike takes you through this beautiful historic garden. From the base of the hill in Old Town, head up through the archaeological digs. Cross the street to see a statue of an idealized Native American, then continue uphill and cross the road at the walkway to see a statue representing a historic padre. Next cross back to the sidewalk and head to the museum. At the base of the museum stairs, an optional path leads behind the building and offers views of the canyon. Once on the museum patio, look through the open archways to the San Diego River. When you're done exploring, head back to your car.

Option: Trek up the stairs to the dirt path that leads through a quiet eucalyptus grove. From there, cross the street again to view the historic cross and then back to the top of the park to wander into a large grassy area, where you might see a couple being married beneath a wooden gazebo. Other paths wind down behind the hill overlooking Old Town to the west or down to the east into the valley below, where you can still discover remains of an old dam and other artifacts. The entire park is riddled with unsigned paths inviting you to explore.

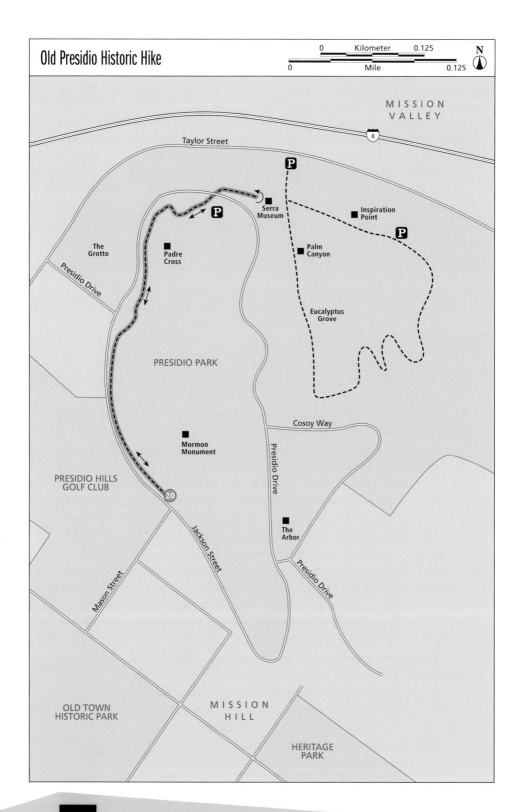

Old Presidio Historic Hike

MISSION VALLEY

0   Kilometer   0.125
0   Mile   0.125

N

Taylor Street

8

P

Serra
Museum

P

The
Grotto

Padre
Cross

Inspiration
Point

P

Palm
Canyon

Presidio Drive

PRESIDIO PARK

Eucalyptus
Grove

Cosoy Way

Mormon
Monument

Presidio Drive

PRESIDIO HILLS
GOLF CLUB

20

Jackson Street

The
Arbor

Presidio Drive

Mason Street

OLD TOWN
HISTORIC PARK

MISSION
HILL

HERITAGE
PARK

MILES AND DIRECTIONS

0.0 Start at the intersection of Mason and Jackson Streets. The trailhead is across the street on the park side. You'll see a path leading to the left and one that goes up a flight of stairs. Take the left trail, which follows the road.

0.1 The trail drifts into the park and away from the road.

0.2 Cross the road to see *The Indian* statue, then cross back to observe the Padre Cross, built from remnants of the old presidio. Continue up the trail.

0.4 Reach the Junipero Serra Museum, which is open on weekends. Explore the park before heading back to the trailhead.

0.8 Arrive back at the trailhead on Mason Street.

Built out of the wreckage of the old presidio, the Padre Cross is a reminder of Spanish settlers.

Otay Valley Regional Park

One of the most popular hiking areas in South County, Otay Valley sits in the heart of National City and yet offers a chance to get away from it all. Dirt paths lead through natural brushland, beside sparkling ponds, and alongside the Otay River. Plans are in the works to connect this intricate web of hikes with Otay Lake to the north and multiuse trails that will lead all the way to the beach.

Start: Trailhead at the end of the crosswalk

Distance: 4.5-mile lollipop

Approximate hiking time: 1.5 hours

Difficulty: Easy

Trail surface: Dirt path

Best season: Year-round

Other trail users: Joggers, people with dogs, equestrians

Canine compatibility: Leashed dogs allowed

Fees and permits: No fees or permits required

Schedule: Open sunrise to sunset; staging area gates open 30 minutes after sunrise to 30 minutes before sunset

Maps: USGS Imperial Beach; trail map available online at www.ovrp .org/documents/ovrpbrochure.pdf

Trail contacts: Otay Valley Regional Park Ranger Station, 2155 Beyer Blvd., San Diego, CA 92154; (619) 424-0463; www .co.san-diego.ca.us/parks/open space/OVRP.html

Finding the trailhead: Take the Main Street exit off I-5. Turn east off the ramp and travel 0.75 mile before turning right onto East Beyer Boulevard. The ranger station is another 0.5 mile. The trailhead is located across the street to the east. GPS: N32.588322 / W117.071605

THE HIKE

Otay Valley is one of San Diego's favorite inland park destinations. With 4.1 miles of multiuse trails meandering through 200 acres of open space that includes seven ponds, glimpses of wildlife, and historical, agricultural, and archaeological resources—all within a quick drive from most of downtown San Diego—it is easy to see the attraction. San Diego is one of the top horse counties in the nation, and you'll see plenty of evidence of that as you walk along the trail. Several trails in Otay Valley link South San Diego Bay with lower Otay Lake.

Plans are in the works to extend the trail system and expand the park's boundaries to broaden the scope of outdoor recreation within southern San Diego County. The new portions of the park will extend within 4 miles of the Mexican border and about 11 miles inland from the southeastern edge of the salt ponds at the mouth of the Otay River to preserve the area around both Lower and Upper Otay Lakes and connect with the San Diego Bay Wildlife Refuge.

Otay Valley is one of the richest in human history. Extensive evidence shows that Native Americans lived here 9,000 years ago, settling in to take advantage of the area's weather and rich natural resources. By the 1800s, Spanish ranchos raised grapes, fruit trees, produce, and cattle in the valley while enjoying the striking views of San Diego Bay, San Miguel, and the Jamul Mountains.

Otay Valley Regional Park has many points of access. While the number of trailheads may confuse new hikers, the simple rule of thumb for hiking in San Diego applies: If a trail looks like it'll take you to a housing development, it probably will. This alone will do a pretty good job of keeping hikers on the right path.

The hike takes you along Otay River for the most part, with stops at several wildlife ponds. Birds can be seen hunting and bathing in the early morning and evening, and small mammals can be seen throughout the day if you are patient. The path is plenty wide for the horses that people ride on this section of the trail.

MILES AND DIRECTIONS

0.0   Start at the Otay Valley staging area on Beyer Boulevard. Cross the street to start the trail.

0.5   Come to the first junction. Take a left and then an immediate right to stay on the main trail.

0.7   Pass under Beyer Way and then stay right to continue on the trail.

0.8   Stay left at the junction.

0.9   Stay right at the junction.

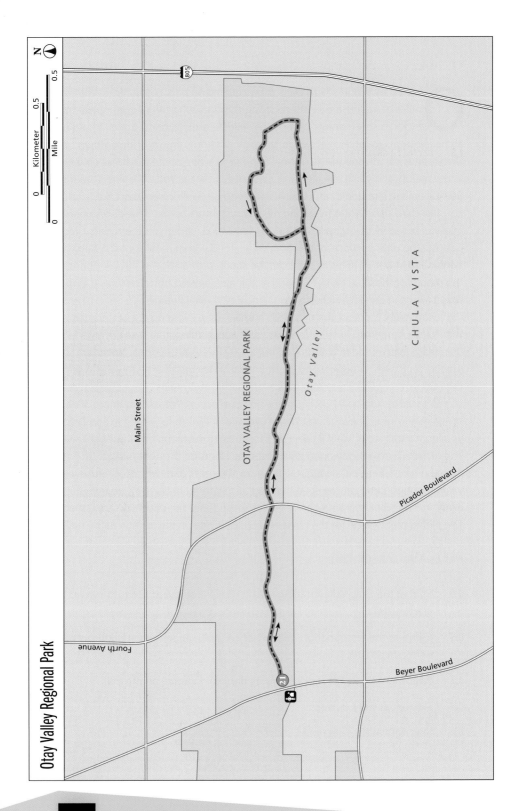

Otay Valley Regional Park

Main Street

OTAY VALLEY REGIONAL PARK

Otay Valley

CHULA VISTA

Fourth Avenue

Picador Boulevard

Beyer Boulevard

805

21

N

Kilometer

Mile

0   0.5

0   0.5

1.1 Stay left as the trail starts to loop around and head back west to continue along the main trail.

2.8 Cross a bridge to arrive again at the previous trail junction and continue on. Bear right to return to the staging area.

4.5 Arrive back at the staging area.

Wrinklebutt and Friends

Hikers who walk along the beaches of the southeastern United States are familiar with fenced-off areas that protect sea turtle nests, but those large turtles aren't a familiar sight on San Diego beaches. Although the cold Pacific waters off San Diego aren't as hospitable as the warmer waters off the country's southeastern Atlantic coast, sea turtles have been sighted in San Diego Bay since the 1850s. How they got there is anyone's guess.

Some speculate that they escaped from seaside "corrals" where they were stored by fishermen who, intending to sell their flesh, brought them back from Mexican waters. Others say the turtles simply migrated north and found a sanctuary in the bay. And still others think the turtles have always been here; they just don't come ashore or nest here, instead spending their summer vacation from warmer Mexican waters meandering north as far as Alaska.

About sixty to one hundred turtles live in the bay today, warmed by the warm waters created by the Duke Energy power plant. All eastern Pacific turtles are endangered, and this is the only location on the West Coast where they gather. The turtles, and the large number of endangered species living in and along the bay, have led the U.S. Fish & Wildlife Service to request that South San Diego Bay be designated as a national wildlife refuge. Studies have shown that the turtles migrate out of the harbor and then swim south more than 1,000 miles to the Revillagigedo Islands off the coast of Mexico to lay their eggs.

But they always return to the warm effluent of the energy plant. The unique waters seem to have a beneficial effect. Turtles in South San Diego Bay are much larger than other populations; in fact, they grow as large as those found in the warm-as-bathwater Caribbean Sea.

The most revered of these resident reptiles is Wrinklebutt. Researchers have been studying this old female (they think) since 1970, and when last measured she weighed in at a whopping 574.2 pounds and stretched out to 3.6 feet when not hiding in her shell. She is the largest eastern Pacific green turtle (also called black turtles) ever documented. Keep up to date on Wrinklebutt and her friends at www.portofsandiego.org/environment/turtle-tracks.html.

Razor Point

Overlooking the sea at the western edge of the continent, Razor Point Trail offers stunning views of the beaches more than 100 feet below. One of several trails within Torrey Pines State Natural Reserve, this hike offers varying views of the ocean all along the way.

Start: Trailhead just to the right of the visitor center's restroom
Distance: 1.7-mile lollipop
Approximate hiking time: 1 hour
Difficulty: Moderate due to some inclines
Trail surface: Dirt path, sand
Best season: Year-round; wild-flowers in spring.
Other trail users: Runners
Canine compatibility: Leashed dogs allowed
Fees and permits: Parking fee
Schedule: 8:00 a.m. to sunset

Maps: USGS Escondido; trail map available online at www .torreypine.org/activities/ hiking-trails-2.html
Trail contacts: Torrey Pines State Natural Reserve, 12600 North Tor-rey Pines Rd., San Diego, CA 92037; (858) 755-2063; www.torreypine .org
Special considerations: Rest-rooms at visitor center. Picnicking only allowed on beach; only water permitted in reserve above beach.

Finding the trailhead: Take I-5 north from San Diego to the Carmel Valley Road exit. Turn left (west) off the ramp and drive toward the ocean for about 1.5 miles until you reach the Pacific Coast Highway (US 101). Turn left onto the Coast Highway and proceed along the beach for about 1 mile. The park entrance is a turnoff on your right just before a large hill. The trailhead is to the right of the visitor center rest-rooms. GPS: N32.9196 / W117.2525

THE HIKE

Climbing proudly over the Pacific Ocean, the sandstone cliffs of Torrey Pines State Natural Reserve culminate in the sharp crux of Razor Point. The area feels more rugged and wild than other parts of the park, due in a large part to the robust varieties of native plant life.

As you first head out you'll quickly transition out of the Torrey pine woodland into the chaparral plant community that frequents the mountain slopes and mesas in the area. Most of these plants are large, dry shrubs with smaller, thick leaves that stay green through multiple seasons. Although more common and dense on the wetter, more north-facing slopes, Nuttall's scrub oak, mountain mahogany, ceanothus, and chamise are all common chaparrals found as you head down the trail.

All chaparral are drought tolerant thanks to various specialized adaptations. Laurel sumac uses its deep, branching root system to find water between rains. The California lilac goes in the opposite direction, with tiny leaves and shallow roots that help it survive extreme water loss. Chaparrals have even developed resilience to California's frequent wildfires and are referred to as "old growth" after seventy-five years. Old-growth chaparral can develop into dense thickets 5 to 15 feet high and serves as shelter for much of the wildlife in Torrey Pines.

As you make your way down the trail you will encounter a form of chaparral that is rare even along the California coastlands—the maritime chaparral. Twisted and bent like an old fisherman, these shrubs have been molded by the ocean

Razor Point juts eagerly into the Pacific Ocean.

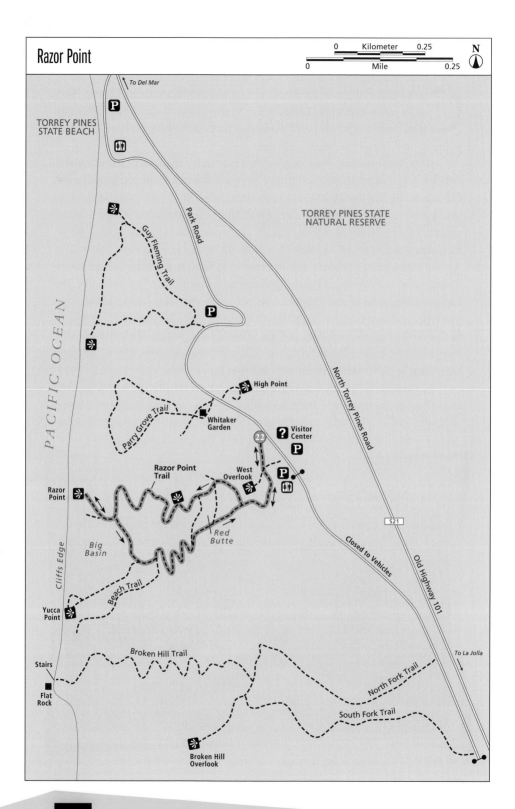

Razor Point

| 0 | Kilometer | 0.25 |
| 0 | Mile | 0.25 |

N

To Del Mar

TORREY PINES
STATE BEACH

Park Road

Guy Fleming Trail

TORREY PINES STATE
NATURAL RESERVE

North Torrey Pines Road

PACIFIC OCEAN

High Point

Parry Grove Trail

Whitaker
Garden

Visitor
Center

West
Overlook

Razor Point
Trail

22

S21

Razor
Point

Red
Butte

Closed to Vehicles

Old Highway 101

Big
Basin

Cliffs Edge

Beach Trail

Yucca
Point

Broken Hill Trail

To La Jolla

North Fork Trail

Stairs

Flat
Rock

South Fork Trail

Broken Hill
Overlook

winds and coastal fogs into striking natural sculptures arcing over the path and the ocean cliffs.

MILES AND DIRECTIONS

0.0   Start from the trailhead and head west. Take a jog onto the scenic overlook before turning around and rejoining the main trail.

0.1   Steer right at the junction.

0.2   Keep right as you cross Red Butte.

0.7   Head right at the junction to reach Razor Point.

0.75 Look down upon all the tiny people far below.

0.8   Return to the junction and turn right.

1.0   Keep left at the junction to stay on the main trail. (**Option:** The side trail to the right leads to Yucca Point.)

1.2   Bear left at the junction with the Beach Trail to stay on the main trail. (**Option:** Turn right onto Beach Trail and hike down to the beaches.)

1.6   Arrive back at Red Butte.

1.7   Keeping right at all remaining turns, arrive back at the trailhead.

Well-traveled paths skirt the edge of the cliffs at Razor Point.

San Diego River Reserve

Following the San Diego River, this hike observes the river as it slowly transitions into an estuary. Numerous birds can be found here year-round. The reserve is a popular biking and hiking destination that takes you off-road from Mission Valley all the way to Dog Beach. Along the way you'll pass under freeways, through estuaries, alongside the river, and into areas seen by few San Diegans.

Start: Sefton Park near Hotel Circle, between the Comfort Suites and Premier Inn

Distance: 3.7 miles point to point

Approximate hiking time: 1 to 2 hours

Difficulty: Easy

Trail surface: Asphalt

Best season: Year-round

Other trail users: Bikers, runners, people with dogs

Canine compatibility: Dogs must be leashed until the beach

Fees and permits: No fees or permits required

Schedule: Reserve open 24 hours

Maps: USGS La Jolla, La Jolla OEW

Trail contacts: City of San Diego Park and Recreation, 202 C Street, MS 37C, San Diego, CA 92101; (619) 236-6643

Special considerations: Don't disturb research areas marked by stakes, poles, flags, or signs. Avoid sensitive sections of boggy or wet areas. Be careful not to step on grassland bird nests. Don't pick flowers, trees, or shrubs; and don't feed, chase, or capture wildlife.

Finding the trailhead: Heading west on I-8, take the exit to Hotel Circle. Turn left onto Hotel Circle North and continue about 0.25 mile until the road dead-ends by Sefton Park between the Comfort Suites and Premier Inn. Park on the street. To find the trailhead, head west along the baseball field rim between the river and the road. GPS: N32.760664 / W117.189885

THE HIKE

The San Diego River begins near Santa Ysabel in East County and runs 52 miles before eventually emptying into the Pacific Ocean at the northern end of Ocean Beach. Along the way it flows through and creates El Capitan Reservoir before gliding through the cities of Santee and San Diego. As the river continues southwest, it traverses Mission Trails Regional Park, where it pours through one of the oldest dams in the West.

Over the course of history, the river has changed paths twice. Sometime in the 1820s the river stopped emptying into Mission Bay and began to drain into San Diego Bay. In 1877 the river was dammed and diverted to ensure that the bay wouldn't be filled with silt. The mouth now divides Ocean Beach and Mission Beach, where it has formed an estuary.

Running through a large city, the San Diego River has some pollution problems. Runoff from streets and homes empties directly into the river, as does trash. However, volunteer groups such as the San Diego River Coalition have done much to restore and protect the river. They organize regular cleanups and work to establish protected areas, such as the Eagle Peak and Mission Valley Preserves. The coalition also works to reduce and eliminate nonnative plant species, as well as acquire and preserve more land.

Abundant grasses surround the flowing water of the San Diego River.

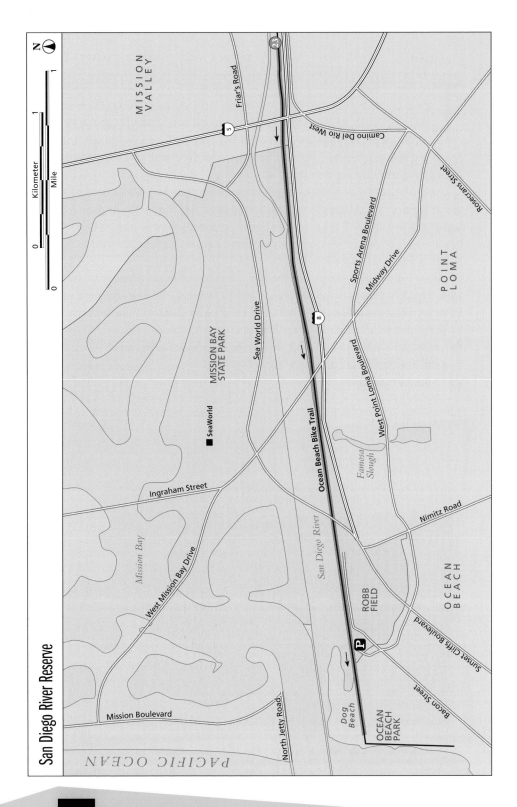

San Diego River Reserve

MISSION VALLEY

Friar's Road

Camino Del Rio West

Rosecrans Street

Sports Arena Boulevard

Midway Drive

POINT LOMA

MISSION BAY STATE PARK

Sea World Drive

■ SeaWorld

Ocean Beach Bike Trail

Famosa Slough

West Point Loma Boulevard

Ingraham Street

Nimitz Road

San Diego River

Mission Bay

West Mission Bay Drive

ROBB FIELD

OCEAN BEACH

Sunset Cliffs Boulevard

Mission Boulevard

North Jetty Road

Dog Beach

Bacon Street

OCEAN BEACH PARK

PACIFIC OCEAN

Kilometer

Mile

N

The trail starts at Sefton Park near Hotel Circle and is a popular bike path. As you move westward toward the ocean, you will pass under several overpasses and watch the trim river become wide and shallow. The trees and shrubs thin out as river grass becomes more dominant. As the river broadens into an estuary, terns and pelicans become common and you can watch them search for shellfish in the delta.

You will pass Robb Field, which offers a superb skate park and athletic fields. The trail culminates when the river hits the ocean at Dog Beach, one of the few leash-free beaches in the country. This section of beach alone makes Ocean Beach one of the best places in San Diego County for dog lovers. After reaching Dog Beach, have someone pick you up or turn around and head back to your car for a 7.4-mile hike.

MILES AND DIRECTIONS

0.0 Start at Sefton Park near Hotel Circle, between the Premier Inn and Comfort Suites.

0.5 Pass under Morena Boulevard, the first of a series of overpasses that you'll go under, including I-5.

2.9 Pass Robb Field Skate Park.

3.7 Arrive at Dog Beach. Play Frisbee with your best friend as you wait for your ride to take you back to your car.

Before leaving Ocean Beach, reward your pickup partner with a meal at Pizza Port at the corner of Santa Monica and Bacon. With the addition of the Ocean Beach store, which opened in May 2010, the local beachside chain is now four strong. Join lots of locals, who sit together to chat, eat, and drink on long picnic tables. Impressive brewed-on-site and selected local craft beers and a wide variety of pizzas include many combinations found at no other restaurant. 1956 Bacon St., Ocean Beach, CA 92107; (619) 224-4700; www.pizzaport.com.

San Dieguito County Park

A favorite destination for families with people of all ages and athletic abilities, this inland retreat offers shady trees, grassy fields, and plenty of play equipment to keep the family busy while you head off for a private stroll. The hike takes you through the most remote areas of the park, down hill and dale to a quiet retreat complete with a small bridge and bubbling brook. Although there is a warren of trails, you can't really get lost—they all head downhill to the grassy lower park.

Start: Upper park entrance on Highland Drive

Distance: 1.2 miles out and back

Approximate hiking time: 1 hour

Difficulty: Moderate

Trail surface: Dirt path

Best season: Year-round

Other trail users: All kinds

Canine compatibility: Leashed dogs allowed

Fees and permits: Parking fee

Schedule: Park open 9:30 a.m. to dusk

Maps: USGS Del Mar; trail maps available online at www.co .san-diego.ca.us/reusable_ components/images/parks/doc/ Trails_San_Dieguito.pdf and www .sdrp.org/trails.htm

Trail contacts: San Dieguito County Park, 1628 Lomas Santa Fe Dr., Del Mar, CA 92014; (858) 755-2386 or (858) 467-4201

Finding the trailhead: From I-5 take the exit for Lomas Santa Fe Drive east. Turn right onto Lomas Santa Fe Drive, then turn left (north) onto Highland Drive and look for the park entrance on your right. Park in the lot and walk across the grassy knoll to the trailhead, located where the hill begins to head down. GPS: N32.997638 / W117.236143

Comprising 125 acres, this county park offers a full spectrum of recreational uses, including expansive lawns, ball fields (including Miracle Field, which accommodates those with special needs), playgrounds, exercise stations, and pavilions and picnic areas, as well as an extensive trail system.

The park is named "Little San Diego" for the rancho of San Diego's first mayor, who claimed 8,000 acres of the best grazing and farming land soon after the area was settled by the Spanish. The land had been designated as Indian settlements, and when the old man died, his son virtually enslaved the natives, who reportedly poisoned him with a mixture of ground human bones and cactus flowers. Rather than suffer an agonizing death, the son shot himself and is said to still roam the area.

Later owners planted the area (and most of Southern California) with eucalyptus trees imported from Australia, thinking the quick-growing trees would provide a source of high-quality lumber. In America, however, the trees became weak and warped. Nonetheless, the distinct scent, papery bark, and delicate branches have become synonymous with Southern California. In addition to the eucalyptus, the park also contains black willow, pepper trees, and pomegranates. Hummingbirds, finches, orioles, and ducks, herons, egrets, and other waterbirds are commonly sighted.

San Dieguito County Park is a great place if you are hiking with little ones. Picnic areas, playgrounds, and open fields give kids of all ages something to do.

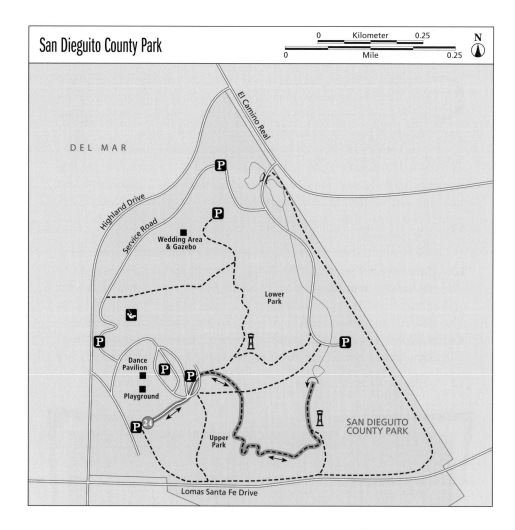

San Dieguito County Park

0 Kilometer 0.25
0 Mile 0.25
N

El Camino Real

DEL MAR

Highland Drive

Service Road

Wedding Area
& Gazebo

Lower
Park

Dance
Pavilion

Playground

Upper
Park

24

SAN DIEGUITO
COUNTY PARK

Lomas Santa Fe Drive

The hike starts from the parking lot directly below the upper park entrance. The grassy park area that you pass over is a popular community destination. Schoolchildren flock here for after-school and summer programs. Just north of where you'll likely be walking is a large dance pavilion where you may see a bride and groom taking their first dance. Continue east over another parking lot to reach the beginning of the natural trail that takes you down the hill.

When you hit a star-shaped junction where several trails meet, take the one on your right. This section of trail takes you through a relatively wild section of the park with trees and moderate inclines. When the wide dirt path begins to bend around back north, you'll see a footpath that continues down through the trees. Take that path.

As the path serpentines up and down, following the natural topography of the land, look for signs of birds, snakes, and small mammals. At one of the bends you will pass a small fortlike tower perched atop the hill. Climb the lookout tower for a great view of the park.

Shortly after the tower, take a smaller side trail that diverges to the left and down the hill. A bubbling brook awaits you as you arrive on the valley floor. Enjoy a nice rest, then turn around and retrace your steps to return to your car.

MILES AND DIRECTIONS

0.0   Start at the upper park entrance on Highland Drive. Proceed directly over the grassy knoll and you'll see a trail leading into the park to your left.

0.3   Turn right at the junction and then go straight at the next one. A few switchbacks will follow shortly.

0.5   Check out the view from the lookout tower.

0.6   Keep on the path before heading left at a side trail to reach the creek. Refresh and head back the way you came.

1.2   Arrive back at the trailhead.

Wide open areas separate the sports facilities at San Dieguito County Park.

San Elijo Lagoon—La Orilla Trail

This remote part of the San Elijo Lagoon takes in the eastern end of the wetland and the watershed that feeds it. Sandy trails merge into packed dirt to wander among towering eucalyptus trees and scrubby hills and into difficult wetlands. Trails criss-cross and interweave as they continue to head west toward the ocean.

Start: Trailhead off El Camino Real
Distance: 2.6 miles out and back
Approximate hiking time: 2 hours
Difficulty: Moderate to difficult
Trail surface: Dirt path
Best season: April through May and August through October, when the annual bird migration is at its peak
Other trail users: Naturalists, critters, anglers, equestrians
Canine compatibility: No dogs allowed
Fees and permits: No fees or permits required

Schedule: Reserve open during daylight hours only; visitor center open 9:00 a.m. to 5:00 p.m. daily except Christmas Day
Maps: USGS Encinitas; trail map available online at www.co.san-diego.ca.us/reusable_components/images/parks/doc/Trails_San_Elijo.pdf
Trail contacts: San Elijo Lagoon Ecological Reserve, 2710 Manchester Ave., Cardiff-by-the-Sea, CA 92007; (760) 634-3026; www.co.san-diego.ca.us/parks/open space/selr.html

Finding the trailhead: From I-5 take the exit for Lomas Santa Fe Drive east, turning right onto Lomas Santa Fe Drive. After about a mile turn left (north) onto Highland Drive at a four-way intersection. At the T intersection turn left onto El Camino Real. Park on the side of the road just before El Camino Real makes a sharp 90-degree right. The trailhead is just off the road through the trees on the right. GPS: N33.009744 / W117.239737

W ith more than 90 percent of California's coastal wetlands destroyed, San Elijo Lagoon Ecological Reserve is among the state's few remaining natural watersheds. One of the most endangered ecosystems in the world, wetlands are a valuable resource because they control erosion, mitigate seasonal flooding, and provide critical habitat for hundreds of species of plants and animals. The San Elijo Reserve has counted 729 species in residence, including Pacific tree frogs and bullfrogs; birds such as widgeons, dowitchers, peeps, avocets, stilts, and Caspian terns; marine and freshwater invertebrates; and a variety of creepy-crawly things like spiders, ants, and praying mantises. Three hundred species of birds live in the lagoon year-round.

The 1,000-acre reserve lies nestled within the embrace of Solana Beach, Encinitas, and Rancho Santa Fe. With 7 miles of trails beginning from eight different trailheads, hikers can experience the biodiversity of six unique plant communities.

The area is a major regional watershed, covering 150 miles of inland drainage from Escondido and La Orilla Creeks that eventually siphon into the estuary. Although development blocked the flow of the estuary for many years, it originally fed to the sea, where it created the rich, sandy beaches Del Mar is known for and created a vibrant, thriving ecosystem. It is a rare ecosystem in recovery.

Marshy wetlands along La Orilla Trail provide birds with places to nest and hide during the day.

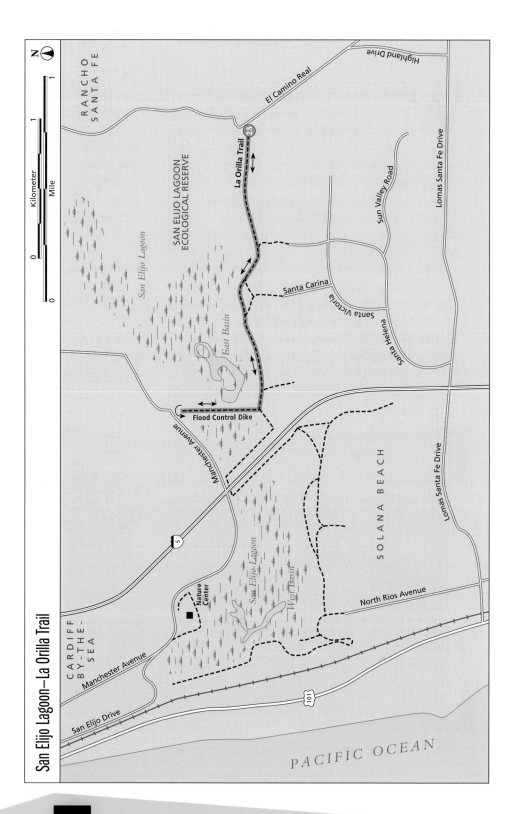

San Elijo Lagoon–La Orilla Trail

The La Orilla Trail starts at the relatively out-of-the-way trailhead on El Camino Real with a lovely trek through tall trees shimmering with dappled light and butterflies. In this riparian woodland, look for wild grape and flowers among the cottonwood and sycamore trees and listen for woodpeckers, song sparrows, and the distinctive buzz of a hummingbird staking its territory. Too soon, the path opens up to chaparral, with only occasional trees for respite. The hike continues along the upper rim of the lagoon, but there are numerous opportunities to take a side trip down to the water, which you can see from your vantage point. This part of the hike is mostly devoid of people, and there's a good chance you won't see anyone else until the lagoon drops below the housing developments.

Paths lead from the housing on your left and are often used by local residents. Continue walking until you hit the levee—a fun jog, since the dirt is hard-packed and straight. The levee will be to your right, behind a gate with a small opening to the left that's plenty big enough for a person but designed to keep wheeled transportation out.

The levee takes you across the lagoon and provides some of the closest views into the heart of the marsh. At the other end of the levee lies Manchester Street, where there's a pullout for a drop-off or pickup but no room for parking.

MILES AND DIRECTIONS

0.0   Start at the La Orilla trailhead off El Camino Real.

0.4   Continue straight through the junction with a trail leading to Santa Helena Street.

0.8   Keep right at the junction with a trail leading to Santa Carina Street.

1.6   Proceed through the gate to walk across the levee. The far end of the levee is your turnaround point. Retrace your steps to return to the trailhead. (**Options:** From here you can have someone pick you up at Manchester Avenue or head back across the levee and continue the trail beneath the overpass.)

3.2   Arrive back at the trailhead.

An Ecological Crisis Averted

San Elijo Lagoon, most of which is shallow-water estuary, is often divided into two main basins that today are separated by I-5, US 101, and the railroad.

The initial arrival of Europeans to the area threatened to destroy the lagoon, once home to an estimated 1,000 Native Americans. First, upland acres were plowed and water used for irrigation, reducing the flow to the sea and introducing nonnative plants and animals.

The rapid development of the twentieth century greatly reduced the water exchange with the ocean, critical to maintaining salinity levels, providing oxygen for marine life, and delivering sand to the beach. At the turn of the century, dikes and levees were introduced to facilitate duck hunting, create sewage settling ponds, and construct a railroad. When the Pacific Coast Highway and I-5 were built, their massive supporting beams appeared to be the epitaph for the lagoon's already fragile existence. Proposals were considered to just fill in the land and build on it. But the lagoon's death throes finally stirred area residents to life.

A small group of local citizens fought for the lagoon to be restored. They wrote letters, set up booths at local festivals, lobbied their political leaders, and educated their neighbors. The group of citizens, scientists, and lawyers formed the San Elijo Alliance and obtained a $1.4 million grant from the Ford Motor Company to help facilitate the restoration. The San Elijo Lagoon Conservancy and the Rancho Santa Fe Foundation also chipped in. Finally, in 2007 the County of San Diego, the State of California, and the San Elijo Lagoon Conservancy signed a twenty-five-year cooperative agreement that officially protected the San Elijo Lagoon Ecological Reserve.

Today, much of the once-endangered tidal flow has been restored by recent combined efforts of the county, state, U.S. Fish & Wildlife Service, and the San Elijo Lagoon Conservancy to dredge the lagoon and allow for greater tidal exchange.

Many people do not realize how strongly the health of tidal wetlands affects the larger coastal ecosystem. Several species of smaller, bait-type fish spawn in estuaries. These fish keep the insect population down and serve as a food source for birds and the larger fish that we humans like to eat.

San Elijo Lagoon—Rios Avenue Trail

This hike explores the basin between I-5 and the railroad tracks, which are no longer functional. The trail is your best bet for seeing birds come home to roost during the twilight hours. The trek east takes you along the hill above the San Elijo Lagoon and continues under the bridge to connect with the La Orilla Trail. Head west to experience the newest sections of trail over the discontinued railroad and to a spur with a comfortable bench that overlooks the lagoon where the wetlands give way to open water.

Start: Pathway at the end of North Rios Avenue

Distance: 1.0-mile lollipop

Approximate hiking time: 30 minutes

Difficulty: Easy

Trail surface: Dirt path

Best season: April through May and August through October, when the annual bird migration is at its peak

Other trail users: Naturalists, critters

Canine compatibility: Leashed dogs allowed

Fees and permits: No fees or permits required

Schedule: Reserve open during daylight hours only; visitor center open 9:00 a.m. to 5:00 p.m. daily except Christmas Day

Maps: USGS Encinitas; trail map available online at www.co .san-diego.ca.us/reusable_ components/images/parks/doc/ Trails_San_Elijo.pdf

Trail contacts: San Elijo Lagoon Ecological Reserve, 2710 Manchester Ave., Cardiff-by-the-Sea, CA 92007; (760) 634-3026; www .co.san-diego.ca.us/parks/open space/selr.html

Finding the trailhead: Take the Pacific Coast Highway (US 101) and turn right onto Lomas Santa Fe Drive east. In 2 blocks turn left (north) onto North Rios Avenue. The road ends at the lagoon. The pathway begins immediately past the end of the street. GPS: N33.003679 / W117.272379

San Elijo Lagoon–Rios Avenue Trail

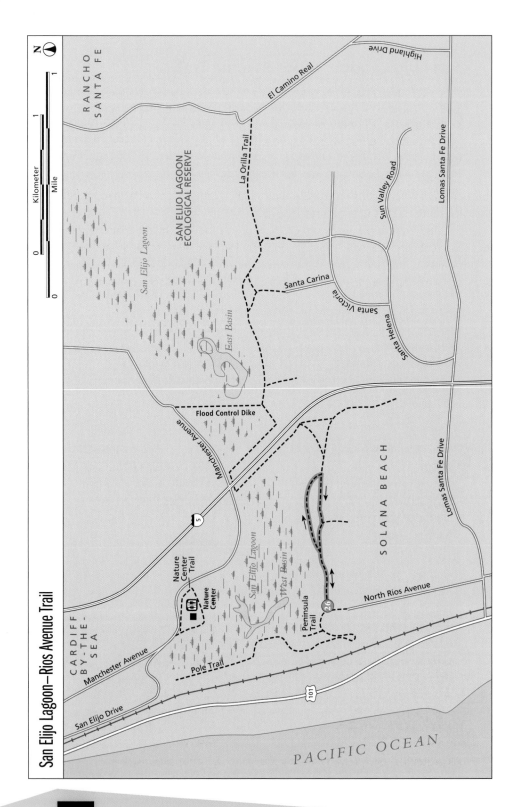

THE HIKE

People first started showing up in what is now San Diego County around 12,000 years ago. Remnants of the peoples who crossed the land bridge from Asia to North American between 14,000 and 47,000 years ago (commonly called Paleo-Indians) moved south as the earth warmed and the ice receded. Two cultures developed as the Paleo-Indians settled into Southern California: the desert culture, which settled inland, and the coastal culture, which stayed near the ocean. The Kumeyaay culture emerged around 1000 CE, categorized by the Ipai culture to the north and the Tipai culture to the south.

The Kumeyaay were reported to have good relations with the Spaniards when Juan Cabrillo first landed in San Diego Bay in 1542 and when Mission San Diego de Alcala was established in 1769. However, they revolted against the new Spanish rule a month after the mission was built. The Spanish population generally stayed

Every Saturday at 10:00 a.m., trained naturalists lead nature walks into the San Elijo Lagoon Ecological Reserve. Just meet at the nature center (2710 Manchester Ave.) to join in. On the second Saturday of each month at 9:00 a.m., guided walks begin at the Rios Avenue trailhead.

Not far from Rios Avenue, views of serene marshland await hikers of the Rios Avenue Trail.

behind their fortified walls, and for the most part the two groups were content with ignoring each other. This dynamic changed when Mexico won its independence from Spain. In 1834 the newly formed government began handing out grants of land formerly owned by the Church. The Kumeyaay were gradually pushed off their land and essentially served as serfs on large ranchos.

The wealth of flora, fauna, and food sources within the lagoon and the watershed that feeds it made it a popular destination for the Kumeyaay. Waterfowl, fish, and edible plants were abundant, and the Kumeyaay used salt from the saltwater marsh to preserve and enhance their food.

Within one-sixth mile around the lagoon, researchers have discovered more than fifty prehistoric sites, although most have been destroyed by development. Within or adjacent to the reserve, there are nineteen prehistoric archaeological sites, including one with both historic and prehistoric components and three historic sites.

Starting from Rios Avenue, the pathway takes you through the saltwater side of the marsh and provides insight into what it was like when the Kumeyaay lived in the area. The trail heads inland, toward the overpass and along the chaparral edge. Heading left from the trail would take you deep into the marsh. The two paths leading to the middle of the marsh are especially popular with birders.

The Rios Avenue Trail takes you on a short loop, and you have the option of continuing east, under the overpass, to connect with the La Orilla Trail. If you're lucky, you might convince a local to show you the secret caves rumored to be within the reserve. Be sure to respect the trails and the lagoon's delicate plant life.

MILES AND DIRECTIONS

0.0 Start at the Rios Avenue trailhead on the south side of San Elijo Lagoon. Take the trail right (east).

0.3 Reach the loop junction. Go left.

0.5 The trail splits. Turn right to complete the loop. (**Option:** Turn left (east) to continue under the overpass and connect with the La Orilla Trail.)

1.0 Arrive back at the trailhead.

Counting Birds: Keeping track of the constantly shifting bird population is more than a full time job, so naturalists ask volunteers to help out. If you're interested, show up at the San Elijo Visitors Center on the second Monday of each month from 7:30 a.m. to noon.

Santa Ysabel Open Space Preserve

One of the region's newest open space preserves, Santa Ysabel offers hikers the chance to see rolling hills covered in purple lupine, grasslands, and mature oak and sycamore trees. With 13 miles of trails within 5,400 acres of wilderness, this preserve offers something for everyone and is well worth the drive from downtown San Diego.

Start: Small parking area just inside the preserve
Distance: 8.5 miles point to point
Approximate hiking time: Full day
Difficulty: Strenuous
Trail surface: Dirt road
Best season: Spring
Other trail users: Equestrians, mountain bikers, wildlife
Canine compatibility: Leashed dogs allowed
Fees and permits: No fees or permits required
Schedule: East Trail open 8:00 a.m. to sunset; West Trail open 8 a.m. to 5 p.m. Friday, Saturday, Sunday, and Monday

Maps: USGS Santa Ysabel; trail map available online at www.sdrp .org/images/syosp%20trails.pdf
Trail contacts: Santa Ysabel Preserves, Farmers Road/Julian Orchards Road, Julian, CA 92036; (760) 765-4098; www.co.san- diego.ca.us/parks/openspace/ Santa_Ysabel.html
Special considerations: No water or facilities on the trail. Trails close for snowfall and half an inch or more of rain until they dry out. Watch for wandering cows. No overnight camping.

Finding the trailhead: From San Diego take I-8 east for approximately 25 miles to CA 79 north. Follow CA 79 north approximately 20 miles into Julian, where it meets CA 78 and becomes Main Street. Head north on CA 78/79/Main Street and then go straight onto Farmer Road when CA 78/79 turns left. Follow Farmer Road 2 miles to Wynola Road and turn right. In less than 500 feet, turn left back onto Farmer Road. Continue about 2 miles. Look for the Santa Ysabel Preserve on your left about 1 mile after passing the Vol- can Mountain Wilderness Preserve sign on your right. Pull into the preserve and park in the staging area. The trailhead is at the end of the small parking area. GPS: N33.34867 / W117.027097

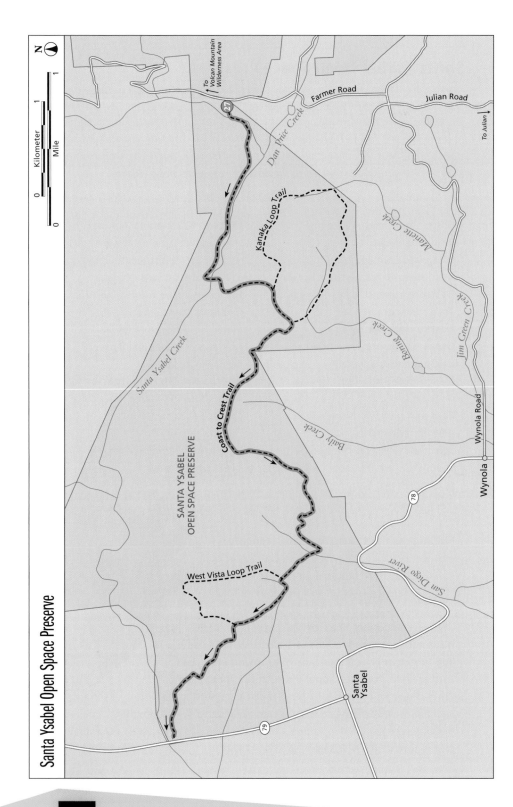

Santa Ysabel Open Space Preserve

THE HIKE

Santa Ysabel Open Space Preserve is a peaceful span of rolling hills, oak forest, and wandering cows and turkeys. The 5,400-acre park contains 13 miles of trails, so it's big enough to be fairly isolated. However, cattle roam freely and often cross the hiking path, which can be intimidating to some. The wild turkey population has grown significantly since the birds were introduced in the Julian-Cuyamaca area in the early '90s.

The preserve is divided by CA 79 into two sections, both of which contain portions of the Coast to Crest Trail, an approximately 55-mile-long trail that extends from Del Mar to Volcan Mountain near the source of the San Dieguito River. The West Trail has much more limited access. The preserve was designed to provide recreation for bicyclists, hikers, and equestrians.

Wildflower lovers can enjoy an array of colors—from white popcorn flowers to pink phlox to abundant purple lupine. The flowers are in bloom from February to June, providing a colorful background to the hills and valleys.

Harsh winds from the mountains sculpt some trees into dramatic shapes.

Following an old dirt access road, the trail climbs in elevation from about 2,930 feet to about 4,300 feet through grassy meadows and mature oak trees. At the peak you will find a pine forest.

Birds, beasts, and bees will be abundant throughout the hike. Possible wildlife sightings include bobcats, bald and golden eagles, California spotted owls, and tricolored blackbirds, as well as deer, cattle, and mountain lions. Part of the area watershed, this isolated sanctuary, with its many creeks and seasonal ponds, is still almost unknown.

Begin your hike at the trailhead, heading west. You'll immediately begin crossing open grasslands that make the sky seem immense. Soon you'll pass under some of the mature oak trees, with trunks large enough to live in. The dappled shade is a welcome relief during hotter times of day.

For almost 1.0 mile the trail follows seasonal Santa Ysabel Creek, whose moisture nurtures sycamore trees and wild blackberries. Continue through the gate, following the Coast to Crest Trail. Numerous picnic tables scattered along the trail make great places to take in the spectacular views of Volcan Mountain and the surrounding territory. The last section, West Vista Loop Trail, includes an optional 1.4-mile loop up the mountain. Continue to the left until you reach the end of the trail at CA 79, where you'll pick up your ride.

MILES AND DIRECTIONS

0.0   Start at the staging area just inside the preserve.

0.3   The trail follows the path of Santa Ysabel Creek.

0.5   Pass under the live oak.

2.2   Pass close to the 4,000-foot peak and follow a bit of the Kanaka Loop for 0.3 mile. (**Option:** Follow the 7-mile Kanaka Loop Trail around the mesa.)

2.5   The trail heads right (west) along the crest of the mountains.

4.2   Pass over the source of the San Diego River.

6.6   At the junction with West Vista Loop Trail, bear left. (**Option:** Turn right to follow a portion of the loop and reconnect with the main trail at 7.4 miles, adding 0.6 mile to your hike.)

6.7   Cross a seasonal mountain stream.

8.5   The hike ends at CA 79. Have someone ready to pick you up.

Wilderness Gardens Preserve—Alice Fries Loop

Head to this 730-acre former farm to enjoy 4 miles of hiking trails, historical and cultural sites, and an interpretive center. The area was once a botanical garden but is slowly transforming back to its native state. In the meantime enjoy wide meadows, a seasonal river, shady forests, and impressive views from mountain summits. Overseen by volunteers and with access restricted by distance and volunteer schedules, this is one of the least-traveled, least-impacted preserves in the county.

Start: Trailhead kiosk just off the parking area

Distance: 0.5-mile loop

Approximate hiking time: 30 minutes

Difficulty: Easy

Trail surface: Dirt path

Best season: After spring rains

Other trail users: Families, picnickers, birders

Canine compatibility: Only assistance dogs allowed

Fees and permits: Parking fee

Schedule: Fri through Mon from 8:00 a.m. to 4:00 p.m.

Maps: USGS Pala; trail map available online at www.co.san-diego .ca.us/reusable_components/ images/parks/doc/Trails_ Wilderness_Gardens.pdf

Trail contacts: Wilderness Gardens Preserve, 14209 Hwy. 76, Pala, CA 92059; (760) 742-1631; www.co.san-diego.ca.us/parks/ openspace/wildernessgardens .html

Special considerations: Bring binoculars, drinking water, sturdy shoes, and a snack.

Other: Picnic tables available

Finding the trailhead: Take I-15 toward North County and exit onto CA 76 east. Drive 10 miles east on CA 76 and look for the park sign on the right. The trailhead begins just off the parking area. GPS: N33.34867 / W117.027097

Wilderness Gardens Preserve–Alice Fries Loop

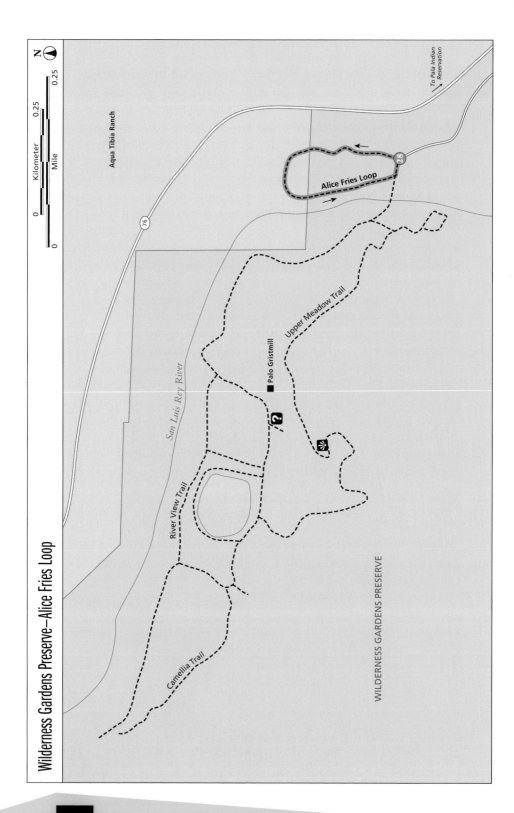

To Pala Indian Reservation

Aqua Tibia Ranch

Alice Fries Loop

28

76

San Luis Rey River

Upper Meadow Trail

Palo Gristmill

River View Trail

Camellia Trail

WILDERNESS GARDENS PRESERVE

N

Kilometer
0   0.25   0.25

Mile
0   0.25

This former ranch became San Diego County's first open space preserve when it was purchased in 1973 from Manchester Boddy, a media mogul who owned the *Los Angeles Daily News*. A horticultural enthusiast, Boddy had landscaped the rich farmland with camellias, azaleas, lilacs, and other shrubs that he sold to friends and neighbors. The county park service is letting the landscaping return to its natural state, eliminating the irrigation system and relying on natural rainfall. Four miles of trails wander throughout the area and around small, unnamed ponds within the rich valley of the San Luis Rey River watershed.

The preserve's trails are restricted to a 100-acre section of the 737-acre park. The public is not allowed off the trails to better preserve habitat for wildlife, including 150 species of wildfowl as well as bobcats, mountain lions, raccoons, and coyotes. The off-limits area is primarily steep and mountainous. The county is trying to connect the gardens to nearby wilderness areas to establish wildlife corridors to facilitate annual migrations.

Located on the outskirts of San Diego County, Wilderness Gardens Preserve provides a retreat for those looking to get away from the crowds.

The best overview of the preserve is found on the Upper Meadow Trail, where you can see the expanse once used for grazing. The pond loop offers a great chance to see wildlife that visits for a quick drink. Camellia Trail offers a hint at the once-well-landscaped gardens. The large camellia bushes along the trail are all that remain from Boddy's 100,000 plantings.

Native terrain is reestablishing itself with woodlands, chaparral, grasslands, coastal sage, and freshwater marsh, as once seen by the Liuseño Indians, who camped in the area annually to gather acorns. Relics of early Native Americans and Spanish settlements, remnants of stagecoach routes, and grinding stones are visible to the discerning eye. The first gristmill in the county was built by the Sickler brothers within the preserve's lands. Now a county historic site, the mill is not within the current trail system.

Head out to this hidden gem of a park to get away from it all. With relatively low traffic, it's possible to explore a wild and wonderful location without your friends and neighbors at your elbow. But get here soon. As its reputation grows, so will its use.

All the trails here are easily accessed, but the quick Alice Fries Loop that heads down toward the river is one of our favorites when the river is flowing. As you follow the loop, look for wildlife, see the valley in its current incarnation across CA 76, and imagine what the area was once like.

MILES AND DIRECTIONS

0.0 Start at the staging area kiosk, heading north on the trail.

0.3 This section of trail is the closest you will get to the river. The seasonal flow depends on recent rains.

0.4 Bear left.

0.5 Arrive back at the staging area. (**Option:** Consider a longer hike through the preserve. Just bear right at every turn and you'll eventually get back to your starting point.)

Peaceful Wilderness Hikes

The cliffs above La Jolla Shores are home to the University of California San Diego and the Scripps Research Institute. See Hike 34.

There is every possibility that while hiking these trails you will have some space between you and the next hiker. While still well within the borders of San Diego County, the hikes in this section are relatively unknown, to newer destinations, challenging enough to discourage the casual hiker, or simply places that people don't recall when they plan to hike San Diego.

Because of their isolation, these are some of our favorite hikes. You can actually hear a seagull screech or see a rare bird being a rare bird—eating, fighting, nesting—as if you were a fellow wild thing instead of one of the invading horde.

San Diego really does have it all for the avid hiker: great weather, unmatched scenery, abundant wildlife, and more than a handful of places where you can be by yourself, especially if you narrow your gaze a bit. The isolated beauty of the Tijuana estuary and its birdlife always gratifies. We've often seen only one or two fellow travelers on these trails. The White Deer Trail is a charming hike as it tells a poignant tale of San Diego's hidden heart. Subtle or obvious, our final trails are magnetic.

Border Field State Park

One of twenty-seven estuarine reserves in the country dedicated to research and education, this 2,500-acre park is fed by 1,735 square miles of watershed. The watershed continues south of the border into Tijuana and Tecate, Mexico. Enjoy mudflats, brackish ponds, and rare vernal pools in this ever-changing habitat filled with life.

Start: Trailhead on the north side of the parking lot

Distance: 1.4 miles out and back

Approximate hiking time: 1 hour

Difficulty: Easy

Trail surface: Paved, dirt path

Best season: Year-round

Other trail users: Dirt bikers, birders

Canine compatibility: Leashed dogs allowed at Border Monument picnic area only

Fees and permits: Entry fee per vehicle

Schedule: Open day after Labor Day to October 31 from 9:30 a.m. to 6:00 p.m.; November 1 to March 14 from 9:30 a.m. to 5:00 p.m.; March 15 to the day before Memorial Day weekend from 9:30 a.m. to 6:00 p.m.; Memorial Day weekend to Labor Day from 9:30 a.m. to 7:00 p.m.

Maps: USGS Imperial Beach; trail map available online at http://trnerr.org/site/?page_id=577

Trail contacts: Border Field State Park, 301 Caspian Way, Imperial Beach, CA 91932; (619) 575-3613; www.tijuanaestuary.org; http://borderfieldstatepark.com

Special considerations: Bring valid ID; the Border Patrol operates an intermittent checkpoint station on Monument Road after the park exit.

Other: During the rainy season, the road often floods and is closed. Check the website (www.trnerr.org/border_field.html) or call (619) 575-3613 between 10:00 a.m. and 5:00 p.m. to see if the gate is open. Equestrian/hiking trails are available on the south end of the Tijuana Estuary. Call ahead for status in case trails are closed due to bad weather.

Finding the trailhead: Take I-5 south to the American side of the Mexican border. Take exit 2 and head southwest about 2 miles on Dairy Mart Road, which will bear right and become Monument Road. Continue right (west) on Monument Road to the park entrance. The trailhead is located on the north side of the parking area. GPS: N32.5428 / W117.1214

THE HIKE

Located at the very southwestern corner of the United States, Border Field is a little-known park within the Tijuana River National Estuarine Research Reserve. The unique saltwater and sand dune ecosystem protects a number of rare birds, including five endangered and two threatened species: the California least tern, the light-footed clapper rail, the California brown pelican, the least Bell's vireo, the Belding's savannah sparrow, the western snowy plover, and the California gnatcatcher. The reserve's critical habitat along the Pacific Flyway earned it a designation as a Globally Important Bird Area by the American Bird Conservancy and a Wetland of International Importance by the Ramsar Convention on Wetlands in 2005. Hawks in particular are abundant here; watch for them as they circle overhead or stand on stately guard over the marshlands.

More than 370 species of birds have been documented hiding within the grassy reeds, skipping up the sand dunes, or wading in the shallow waters. The area includes five distinct ecosystems: salt marsh, upland, cacti and succulents, beaches and dunes, and riparian areas.

The deceptively still landscapes of Border Field State Park are full of life.

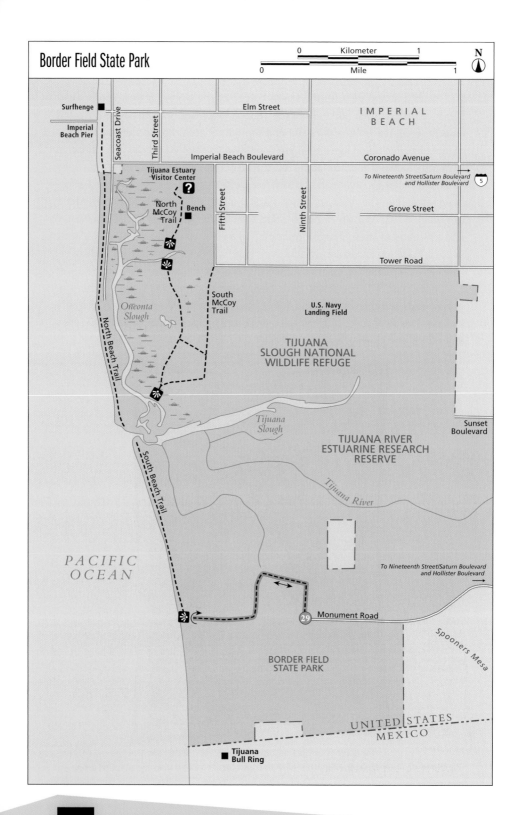

Border Field State Park

0 Kilometer 1
0 Mile 1

N

Surfhenge
Imperial Beach Pier
Seacoast Drive
Third Street
Elm Street
IMPERIAL BEACH
Imperial Beach Boulevard
Coronado Avenue
To Nineteenth Street/Saturn Boulevard and Hollister Boulevard
5
Tijuana Estuary Visitor Center
North McCoy Trail
Bench
Fifth Street
Ninth Street
Grove Street
Tower Road
South McCoy Trail
Oneonta Slough
U.S. Navy Landing Field
TIJUANA SLOUGH NATIONAL WILDLIFE REFUGE
North Beach Trail
Tijuana Slough
Sunset Boulevard
TIJUANA RIVER ESTUARINE RESEARCH RESERVE
South Beach Trail
Tijuana River
PACIFIC OCEAN
To Nineteenth Street/Saturn Boulevard and Hollister Boulevard
29
Monument Road
Spooners Mesa
BORDER FIELD STATE PARK
UNITED STATES
MEXICO
Tijuana Bull Ring

In addition to hikers, you'll encounter equestrians, birders, and beachcombers (who may look at but must not keep their prizes), although swimming and wading are restricted because of hazardous currents. As you walk through the coastal dunes that were once common up and down the California coast, you will be wandering a disappearing ecosystem, much of it bulldozed under to create hundreds of miles of human habitat. The fragile dunes host plants that cannot grow anywhere else. As you walk toward the beach, stay off the dunes—they are as endangered as their inhabitants.

When you reach the shore, head either north or south along the beach before backtracking to your car.

This may be the loneliest beach in California. Look for dolphins frolicking in the water and horses dipping their hooves in the only beach in the county where they are allowed. During migration season, California gray whales can be seen heading to or from Mexico for the breeding season. Don't mention this to your

The Ramsar Convention on Wetlands (ramsar.org) is a global environmental treaty devoted to protecting the world's most important wetlands as areas of critical importance to the health of the planet.

Shrubbery is a haven for birds at Border Field State Park, part of an internationally recognized wildlife preserve.

friends, though. We like the opportunity to be the only ones on the beach. Head back to your car along Monument Road.

MILES AND DIRECTIONS

0.0 Start at the equestrian staging area where Monument Road turns due south. Head due north along an equestrian/hiking trail.

0.1 Turn left and follow the trail west toward the ocean.

0.2 Turn left again as the trail turns south. Take a moment to look for the endangered least tern or California brown pelican.

0.5 The trail rejoins the Horse Trail along Monument Road. Turn right and head toward the beach through coastal dunes.

0.7 Arrive at the beach, your turnaround point. Retrace your steps back to the trailhead. (**Option:** Enjoy an isolated coastal walk before heading back to your car.)

1.4 Arrive back at the trailhead.

Canyon Cleanup

Members of WiLDCOAST meet on Saturday to give environmental seminars to residents of Cañon de los Laureles in Tijuana to teach them about recycling and composting. The area is without trash and recycling services, and almost ten million plastic bottles and 4,000 tires get dumped into the Tijuana River Valley each year, blackening the water artery and polluting the ocean.

Cañones Limpios (Clean Canyons) helps Mexicans be more friendly to the environment by pooling resources and coordinating truck trips to recycling plants. WiLDCOAST also collects tons of tires every year with biannual trash collection parties that coordinate with San Diego's Allied Waste to haul the collection away. In October 2010 a month-long cleanup yielded fifty-six tons of trash.

To join the effort or find out about other projects, contact WiLDCOAST, 925 Seacoast Dr., Imperial Beach, CA 91932; (619) 423-8665; www.wildcoast .net/; e-mail: volunteers@wildcoast.net.

Cabrillo Monument Bayside Trail

Dripping with history, the Bayside Trail at Point Loma offers so much more than just a gorgeous walk. From the whale lookouts to the artillery bunkers, this is a place to satisfy even the pickiest of adventurers. Take the time to tour the visitor center to learn more about the point's unique history as well as its exceedingly rare ecosystem. The hike takes you through one of the last remaining coastal scrublands in the world.

Start: Visitor center parking lot

Distance: 2.8 miles out and back

Approximate hiking time: 1.5 hours

Difficulty: Moderate due to inclines

Trail surface: Paved road, dirt path

Best season: Winter, when temperatures are at their coolest and whales frolic in the ocean

Other trail users: Whale watchers in season, birders, moms, and kids

Canine compatibility: No dogs allowed

Fees and permits: Entry fee

Schedule: Monument open 9:00 a.m. to 5:00 p.m. For security purposes, the entrance station closes at 4:30 p.m., the main gate into Cabrillo National Monument closes at 4:45 p.m., and all visitors must exit the park by 5:00 p.m. The park asks that visitors be off the trail by 4:00 p.m.

Maps: USGS Point Loma; trail map available online at www .nps.gov/cabr/planyourvisit/ loader.cfm?csModule=security/ getfile&PageID=21254

Trail contacts: Cabrillo National Monument, 1800 Cabrillo Memorial Dr., San Diego, CA 92106; (619) 557-5450; www.nps.gov/cabr

Other considerations: The park closes at 5:00 p.m., so come early. The tip of Point Loma is under control of the military, and a gate guard ensures that no one accesses the point without a pass after 5:00 p.m.

Finding the trailhead: Located at Point Loma, Cabrillo National Monument is within the San Diego city limits. Take I-8 west to the Rosecrans Street/CA 209 exit, then travel about 2.5 miles on Rosecrans Street before turning right onto Canon Street. Turn left onto Catalina Boulevard and follow the signs to the park and visitor center. The paved trail heads downhill between the visitor center and the lighthouse. GPS: N32.6742 / W117.2409

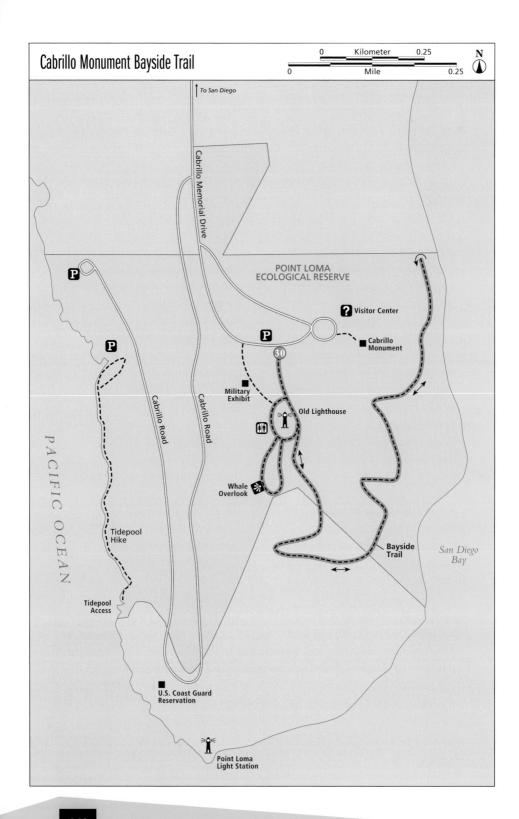

Cabrillo Monument Bayside Trail

0 Kilometer 0.25

0 Mile 0.25

N

↑ To San Diego

Cabrillo Memorial Drive

P

P

POINT LOMA
ECOLOGICAL RESERVE

? Visitor Center

P

■ Cabrillo
Monument

30

Military
Exhibit

Cabrillo Road

Cabrillo Road

Old Lighthouse

Whale
Overlook

Bayside
Trail

*San Diego
Bay*

PACIFIC OCEAN

Tidepool
Hike

Tidepool
Access

■ U.S. Coast Guard
Reservation

Point Loma
Light Station

THE HIKE

Cabrillo National Monument is dedicated to the man many historians believe to be Spain's last great explorer: Juan Rodriguez Cabrillo. The first European to sail along the western coast of North America, Cabrillo explored and charted what is now San Diego in an effort to discover a spice route to Asia, claim land for Spain, search for gold, and discover the rumored Strait of Anian, part of the legendary Northwest Passage.

The exact place of Cabrillo's birth and death are unknown, as is his gravesite, but the period of his life in the Americas prior to his northern expedition is well documented. He came to the Americas in 1520 as a soldier and invaded the Aztec city of Tenochtitlan under Hernando Cortez. From there Cabrillo used his education to become one of the wealthiest landowners in what was then New Spain, with businesses ranging from gold prospecting to ship building. In 1542 Cabrillo set sail on an expedition to "discover the coast of New Spain" under the commission of the new viceroy. In addition to his explorations up the coast of California, he befriended the local Kumeyaay Indians before dying of what was most likely infection in 1542 somewhere around Catalina Island. Records from his expedition were lost.

Before being decommissioned, the old Point Loma Lighthouse guided ships into the harbor for thirty-six years.

The Bayside Trail is a must if you plan on visiting Point Loma. Be sure to stop by the visitor center for information (ask about the old lighthouse) before heading up to the small loop around the lighthouse. In January and February gray whales can be seen off the coast during their 12,000-mile migration. In the bay to the east is the U.S. Navy training ground, where they train in submarine and antisubmarine warfare.

Heading down the path toward the bay, you'll find remnants of Point Loma's past as a harbor defense during World Wars I and II. During this time the lighthouse was painted green and used as a radio tower. Frequent signs describe native plants along the trail.

The windblown promontory is home to one of the last coastal scrublands on the planet. The 422-foot ridge falls rapidly down to the bay on one side and the ocean on the other. Four unique microsystems exist within the landscape: southern coastal bluff scrub, maritime succulent scrub, Diegan coastal sage scrub, and southern maritime chaparral. During the hike you'll see agave, coastal poppy, Indian paintbrush, snake cholla, and prickly pear cactus among other native plants typical of a coastal Mediterranean ecosystem. The steepness of the hike keeps it relatively isolated. If you are lucky you might see foxes or coyotes hidden amidst the bushes or a red-tailed hawk seeming to float in place as it looks for shrews, mice, and lizards brave enough to hazard the open.

The hike is of moderate length and steepness, while the view of the bay is unsurpassed. Please stay on the trail, as the area is an ecological conservation area. There is an ongoing effort in San Diego to set aside such places in order to protect the hundreds of native species that are endangered or threatened.

MILES AND DIRECTIONS

0.0 Start from the visitor center parking lot, following the sidewalk that leads to the lighthouse.

0.1 Arrive at the junction with the lighthouse loop. Bear right onto the loop around the lighthouse and take a quick peek at the Whale Overlook.

0.5 Nearing completion of the lighthouse loop, arrive at a junction with an access road. Turn right and proceed downhill on the paved access road leading to the Bayside Trail.

0.8 The well-marked path diverges from the road on the left.

1.4 The trail ends at an area closed off as an ecological reserve. Enjoy the climb as you retrace your steps, heading right to return to the visitor center.

2.8 Arrive back at the trailhead.

Carlsbad Beach

Bordered by spectacular beaches on the one side and spectacular private homes on the other, this lagoon-to-lagoon walk gives you an idea how the other half lives as you imagine your own private beachfront abode. The excursion takes you through wide, relatively isolated beaches populated primarily by local residents and offers two optional excursions into recovering lagoons. As you head south you'll move from flat beach areas to San Diego's towering cliffs that butt against the shore. This is truly a spectacular barefoot hike.

Start: Parking lot at Buccaneer Park
Distance: 5.0 miles out and back
Approximate hiking time: 2.5 hours
Difficulty: Moderate due to length
Trail surface: Sand
Best season: Winter, when the beaches are empty and there is a chance to glimpse migrating whales
Other trail users: Beachgoers, surfers, summer campers, pelicans
Canine compatibility: No dogs allowed on beach; leashed dogs allowed on the walkways above the beach
Fees and permits: No fees or permits required for day use
Schedule: Daylight hours year-round
Maps: USGS San Luis Rey; trail map available online at www.californiacoastaltrail.info/hikers/hikers_main.php?DisplayAction=DisplaySection&CountyId=20&SectionId=419
Trail contacts: North Sector Superintendent, California State Parks Department; (760) 720-7001; www.parks.ca.gov/parkindex/region_info.asp?id=10&tab=1 Carlsbad City Hall, 1200 Carlsbad Village Dr., Carlsbad, CA, 92008; (760) 434-2820
Special considerations: Lifeguard towers are open 10:00 a.m. to 6:00 p.m. during the summer season (late June to Labor Day)
Other: No portable grills, alcohol, smoking, or glass containers allowed. This hike is best enjoyed during low tide.

Finding the trailhead: From I-5 north at the northernmost end of Carlsbad, take the exit for Vista Way, turning left (west) off the exit. Three blocks past the Coast Highway, turn right (north) on Broadway and then left (west) on Cassidy Street to cross the railroad tracks. Turn right (north) on South Pacific Street and continue until it runs into Buccaneer Park on your right, on the corner of Morse Street. From the parking lot at Buccaneer Park, head to the beach and go left (south). GPS: N33.17701 / W117.368387

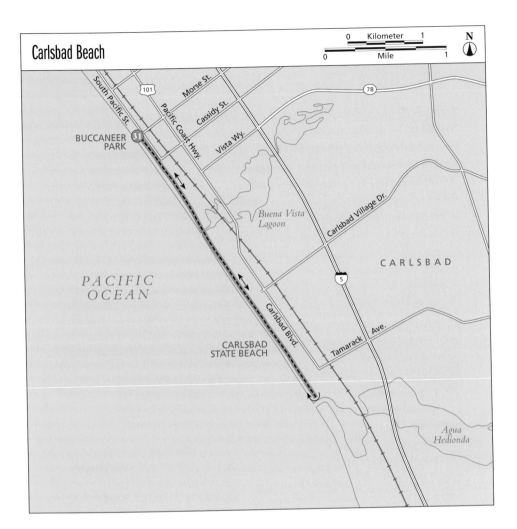

Carlsbad Beach

Buccaneer Park

Morse St.

Cassidy St.

Vista Wy.

101

South Pacific St.

Pacific Coast Hwy.

78

PACIFIC
OCEAN

Buena Vista
Lagoon

Carlsbad Village Dr.

CARLSBAD

5

Carlsbad Blvd.

CARLSBAD
STATE BEACH

Tamarack Ave.

Agua
Hedionda

THE HIKE

This hike begins on Oceanside's southernmost beach and takes you to Carlsbad's northernmost beach. Although the beaches are not private, there are not many public access points, so the walk from Buccaneer Park to Agua Hedionda Lagoon can be relatively private. Along the way you'll see a few public entry points, but if you don't own one of the impressive homes along this stretch of beach, you have to hike a bit to get to the beach. Man-made rock barriers protect the homes from erosion, but waterside the sand is pristine and the likelihood of seeing wildlife is boosted by the lack of crowds. During high tide, the beach can disappear, forcing walkers onto the rocky barriers if they linger long enough. So watch for high tide and check tide maps to ensure that you can actually hike along the shore.

The beaches between Oceanside and Pine Avenue are owned jointly by the homeowners and the state. Because the beaches don't offer lifeguards, restrooms, or other amenities, this stretch of beach is often empty. Hikers, surfers, and families who meander out from their homes compete with sandpipers, pelicans, and curlews for beach space.

The hike begins at Buccaneer Beach, a small beach dedicated to swimmers, waders, and body boarders. This is the last lifeguard tower for a while, so get your ocean dip here before heading south. The homes that line the seashore are as eye-popping as the sea and showcase the epitome of beachside living. As you walk along you will see homes of every shape and style. The beach itself is what Californians love most: wide, white sand that stretches for miles.

North County coastal business and community leaders created the Ruddy Duck Club to support nature education and recreation programs offered at the Buena Vista Audubon Nature Center. For further information call (760) 439-2473.

Murals under an overpass highlight Buccaneer Park's artistic flair.

When you get to Buena Vista Lagoon, you can take an optional hike alongside the lagoon waters into the ecological reserve to look for additional onshore birds and wildlife, including marbled godwits, sanderlings, California thrashers, vermilion flycatchers, and numerous hummingbirds.

Continuing along the beach, you pass from Oceanside into Carlsbad (don't bother to look for markers; there won't be any). You can tell that you've reached Carlsbad State Beach when the houses end. Continue along the state beach or pop up to the walkway that runs along the length of the beach until you reach Agua Hedionda Lagoon, another possible excursion with myriad trails. If you look inland along the water's edge, you'll see the Hubbs-Seaworld Research Institute. Return the way you came, noting that people-watching opportunities change depending on the time of day. After completing your hike, enjoy a well-deserved drink in one of Carlsbad's quaint local restaurants along the Coast Highway.

MILES AND DIRECTIONS

0.0 Start at the parking lot and head to the beach, turning south. (**Option:** For a shorter hike, use one of the public access points at Carlsbad Village Drive, Grand Avenue, Christiansen Way, Beech Avenue, or Rue des Chateaux.)

1.0 Cross the mouth of the stream where Buena Vista Lagoon empties into the ocean.

1.8 Carlsbad State Beach begins.

2.5 The hike ends at Agua Hedionda Lagoon where the lagoon meets the sea. Return the way you came.

5.0 Arrive back at the trailhead.

For Gardeners

Get to know native and drought-tolerant plants through the Buena Vista Native Plant Club, which meets the third Saturday of the month at the nature center. Events include planting advice, cutting exchanges, plant sales, and field trips as well as regular tours of gardens that feature native plants.

The center offers a list of landscape designers who specialize in native plant gardens, as well as free compost for Oceanside residents (nonresidents pay a modest fee.) The club meets at the Buena Vista Audubon Nature Center, 2202 South Coast Hwy., Oceanside. Call (760) 439-2473 for more information.

Imperial Beach Pier

The southernmost beach town in the United States offers wide, uncrowded beaches; frequent dolphin visits; and a newly vibrant beach community. The poor stepchild of San Diego beach communities, Imperial Beach is now asserting its mojo with an increasing reputation as a surfing, sand castle–building, environmental mecca.

Start: Imperial Beach Pier
Distance: 3.3 miles out and back
Approximate hiking time: 2 hours
Difficulty: Easy
Trail surface: Sand
Best season: Year-round
Other trail users: Beachgoers, runners
Canine compatibility: No dogs allowed
Fees and permits: No fees or permits required
Schedule: Pier closed between 10:00 p.m. and 5:00 a.m.

Maps: USGS Imperial Beach OEW; trail maps available online at www.californiacoastaltrail.info/hikers/hikers_main.php?DisplayAction=DisplaySection&CountyId=21&SectionId=409 and www.californiacoastaltrail.info/hikers/hikers_main_horizontal.php?DisplayAction=DisplaySection&CountyId=21&SectionId=411
Trail contacts: City of Imperial Beach, 425 Imperial Beach Blvd., Imperial Beach, CA 91932-2601; (619) 628-1385
Imperial Beach Pier, 2 Elder Ave., Imperial Beach, CA 91932

Finding the trailhead: From I-5 south take exit 5A (CA 75/Palm Avenue), turning left (west) off the exit. Turn left onto Palm Avenue as CA 75 heads north up the strand. Turn left onto Seacoast Drive just before you reach the coast and then turn right onto Elder Avenue. Follow Elder until you hit the beach (1 block). There is limited parking 1 block north on Evergreen, but you may get lucky. Otherwise park on a side street and walk back to the pier, heading south once you get on the beach. GPS: N32.579508 / W117.132601

This laid-back beach town celebrated its fiftieth anniversary in 2006 with typically low-key enthusiasm. Town residents are torn between pride of place and the desire to keep one of best-kept secrets on the West Coast from becoming a frenzied tourist destination like so many of her sisters. Wide-open park space, two-story condos, and private homes line the beach when it isn't silhouetted by swaying palm trees.

As you hike south, watch the delicate dance between local surfers and the ocean waves. Imperial Beach is known for its big waves. In fact, it was a major destination for early mainland surfers. Surfing pioneers from 1937 through the 1950s headed to IB to surf the volatile waves that broke just outside the delta at the mouth of the Tijuana Slough. Dempsey Holder was known as the Dean of the Sloughs and helped propel IB into a premier surfing destination.

Surfhenge, a neon representation of surfboards, marks the entrance to the city's major park and pier. Colorful surfboard benches with accompanying plaques tell the stories of key surfers, many of whom made the trek to IB to surf the biggest known waves off the coast of the continental United States. Begin your hike by passing under *Surfhenge* before heading south at the pier along some of the best sand on the coast.

Even during the busiest times, these beaches seem wide open and empty. Surfers enjoy long, slow waves populated by the occasional dolphin pod. Imperial Beach Boulevard (a parking area butts up against the beach) marks the end of the town center. South of this point, development consists of beachfront homes and condos a block deep that are bordered by the ocean on one side and Seacoast Drive on the other.

To the east of Seacoast, the Tijuana Slough takes over. There are only three additional public access points between here and the last of the development before the slough and the beach collide. At high tide you may have to climb on the rocky seawall to keep dry.

From here on, it is only wild sea, sand, sun, and slough. Rare coastal dunes harbor endangered least tern nesting grounds. The Oneonta Slough empties into the ocean and marks the border between the United States and Mexico. Crossing the border here into Mexico is illegal, as is crossing the border from Mexico into the United States, but this was once a common crossing area, with immigrants trying to swim up the coast or up the slough. Now most border crossings have moved inland, and Imperial Beach and its wide, white sand see more activity from wildlife than humans. Still, Border Patrol is active here 24/7.

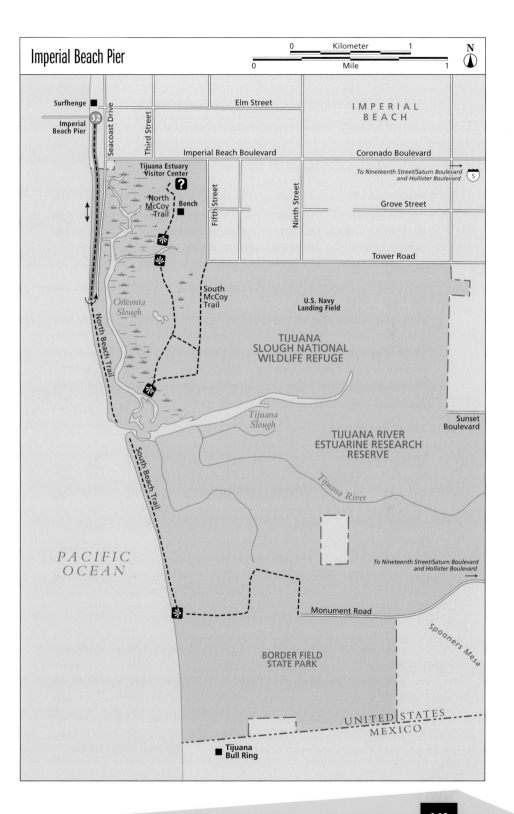

0.0 Start at *Surfhenge,* passing under the unique sculpture.

0.1 Dunes Park ends. Low-structured housing begins to line the beachfront.

0.2 As the beach narrows, you will see stone seawalls, built to protect homes during high tide and storms.

0.3 Reach a public access point, one of many appearing along the beach. (Unlike many beach communities, public access ways are available at almost every block.) Development is limited to one row of houses tucked between the slough and the sea with access via Seacoast Drive.

1.0 Development ends.

1.65 Walk the wild dunes to the border of Mexico. Turn around here and retrace your path. (**Options:** Just south of the first house you meet on your way back, you can cross inland to access a boardwalk overlooking an estuary on the east side of Seacoast Drive. Follow the estuary north for as long as you like or until it meets housing development. From there, you can cross back to the beach using any of the multiple beach access points or continue along Seacoast Drive back to the pier.)

3.3 Arrive back at the trailhead.

Hunting for Grunion

Many people think grunion hunting is akin to snipe hunting. After all, you have to go out at midnight, bring nothing but your hands and a catch bucket, and trust to the moon and the tides to bring the grunion.

But the grunion run is far from mythical. The small fish swarm onto the beach to lay eggs and spawn in the spring and summer when the moon is just right. "Hunters" scramble to scoop up as many of the tiny silver-sided fish as they can by hand. (You'll need a license if you are over sixteen.)

A hike by moonlight to watch the run is a guaranteed memory-maker. For a current schedule, send a self-addressed, stamped envelope to GRUNION, California Department of Fish and Game Marine Region, 4665 Lampson Ave., Suite C, Los Alamitos, CA 90720.

Sand Castles and Surfing Dogs

Imperial Beach hosts the largest sand-sculpting competition in the United States, the U.S. Open Sandcastle Competition. The whimsical sculptures line the beach along Pier Plaza and Seacoast Drive. IB's own ten-man team, the IB Posse, has been competing for years, often winning the $5,000 cash prize. Contact the U.S. Open Sandcastle Committee, Inc., P.O. Box 476, Imperial Beach, CA 91933; (619) 424-6663; www.usopensandcastle.com.

The pier also is home to the Annual Loews Coronado Bay Resort Surf Dog Competition. Dogs compete by weight and without human companions. The competition attracts dog owners from around the country, whose dogs may take lessons from the Coronado Surfing Academy before the event. The competition is a fund-raiser for pet-related charities. Call (619) 424-4474 or visit www.loewssurfdog.com for sponsorship or competition information.

The San Diego skyline greets you as you travel up Imperial Beach.

Kwaay Paay Peak

A steep ascent takes you 800 feet above the valley floor, revealing the entire Mission Trails Park. Kwaay Paay Peak is more centralized and more accessible than Cowles Mountain yet also offers fantastic views. The hike takes you though sagebrush and flowering native plants before you reach the summit, from which you can look down on an old quarry.

Start: Parking lot at the old mission dam
Distance: 2.1 miles out and back
Approximate hiking time: 2 hours
Difficulty: Strenuous
Trail surface: Dirt path
Best season: Year-round
Other trail users: None
Canine compatibility: Leashed dogs allowed
Fees and permits: No fees or permits required

Schedule: Sunrise to sunset
Maps: USGS La Mesa; trail map available online at www.sandiego .gov/park-and-recreation/pdf/ missiontrailstrailmap.pdf
Trail contacts: Mission Trails Regional Park, 1 Father Junipero Serra Trail, San Diego, CA 92119; (619) 668-3281; www.mtrp.org
Special considerations: Take water; it gets hot up there.

Finding the trailhead: From I-5, I-805, CA-163, or I-15, take CA 52 east, heading toward Santee. Take the Mast Boulevard exit in Santee, turning left onto Mast Boulevard. After passing under the freeway, take the first right onto West Hills Parkway, then take the first right onto Mission Gorge Road. Drive 0.2 mile and then turn right onto Father Junipero Serra Trail. Continue 0.7 mile and park in the lot at the entrance to Old Mission Dam, on the right. From the parking lot, cross the street and find the path that heads uphill. GPS: N32.839548 / W117.041245

THE HIKE

The Old Mission Dam that greets you at the trailhead parking lot is another remnant from the early Spanish pioneers who settled and controlled Southern Californian for hundreds of years until the Mexican-American War. Finally completed in 1815, the dam has its own long and vivid history.

When the Spanish missionaries arrived in 1769 along with the Mexican army, they settled in a location overlooking the San Diego River that they shared with the soldiers for almost five years. In 1774 the padres, feeling they'd be better off on their own, left the Royal Presidio to settle 6 miles upriver.

Searching for a reliable long-term water source, the padres found a suitable dam site in what is today Mission Gorge. However, it wasn't until 1809 that labor and other resources were in sufficient supply to begin construction. It took six years using mostly local Indians to construct the dam and supporting flume, each a tremendous task in itself. The completed dam was 13 feet thick, 244 feet long, and built on top of exposed bedrock. From there the water flowed through the spill-ways to the 3-mile-long aqueduct over gulches, hills, and gaps up to 15 feet wide until it finally reached the mission. The flume provided water to the mission until 1833, when California missions were secularized. No longer maintained, the flume was gradually destroyed by natural flooding and scavenged by pioneers looking for building materials.

Kwaay Paay Trail is rugged and long, built for only the brave and strong.

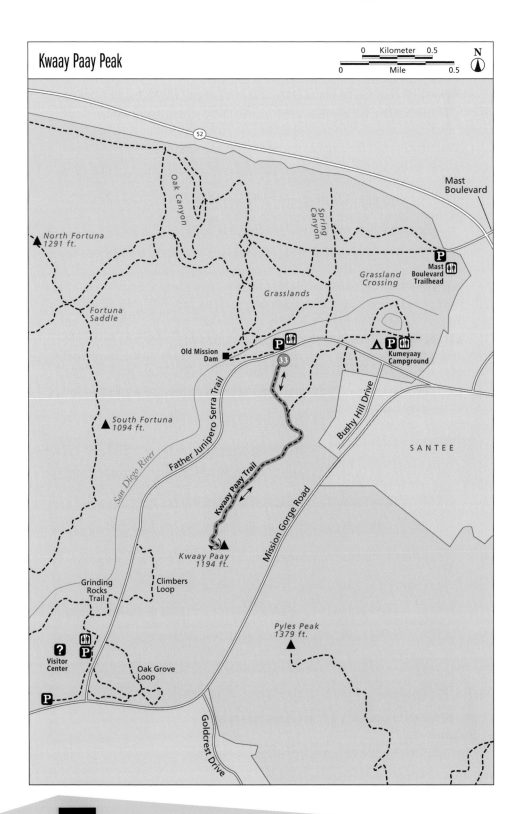

Kwaay Paay Peak

0 Kilometer 0.5
0 Mile 0.5

N

52

Mast Boulevard

Oak Canyon

Spring Canyon

North Fortuna
1291 ft.

Grassland Crossing

P

Mast Boulevard Trailhead

Grasslands

Fortuna Saddle

Old Mission Dam

P

33

P

Kumeyaay Campground

South Fortuna
1094 ft.

San Diego River

Father Junipero Serra Trail

Bushy Hill Drive

SANTEE

Kwaay Paay Trail

Mission Gorge Road

Kwaay Paay
1194 ft.

Grinding Rocks Trail

Climbers Loop

Pyles Peak
1379 ft.

?

Visitor Center

P

Oak Grove Loop

P

Goldcrest Drive

The trip up Kwaay Paay Peak is shorter than it feels like but at least as steep. The cantankerous chaparral converges into a dense thicket as you near the top, and animal trails dart through the underbrush and across the trail. The trail steepens even further as the summit comes into view, and in many places steps are added to ease the ascent.

When you finally reach the peak, Mission Valley unfolds before you. Enjoy the view of the old quarry below you and the visitor center at the far end of the park. Take the time to catch your breath and make a leisurely exploration of the various trails and nontrails along the summit. None of the trails lead anywhere and are best for a brief stroll before heading back the way you came.

MILES AND DIRECTIONS

0.0 Start at the Kwaay Paay trailhead, across the road from the Old Mission Dam parking lot. (**Option:** Enjoy the dam before heading to the trailhead.)

0.3 Keep right at the junction to Kumeyaay Lake.

0.8 The path becomes very steep and sometimes slippery. Watch your step.

1.1 Arrive at the summit. Enjoy the wide-open view of the area before heading back down the mountain.

2.2 Arrive back at the trailhead.

La Jolla Shores to Black's Beach

Wide beaches, tide pools, an observation pier, and the Scripps Institution of Ocean-ography are all reasons to explore this stretch of coast. Whether drawn to the famous white sands and surf culture of San Diego at La Jolla Shores or to the more infamous Black's Beach, you're sure to love what you find. However, the long, broad stretches of beach under the looming sea cliffs might be the best draw of all.

Start: Kellogg Park
Distance: 2.4 miles point to point
Approximate hiking time: 1 to 2 hours
Difficulty: Moderate due to some rocks and steep stairs at the gli-derport
Trail surface: Sand, rocks
Best season: Year-round
Other trail users: Photographers, scientists, scuba divers, snorkelers, college students, nudists, natural-ists, extremely rich residents who can afford a private tram to their private beach house
Canine compatibility: Leashed dogs allowed from 6:00 p.m. to 9:00 a.m. only. (You must clean up after your pet.)

Fees and permits: No fees or per-mits required
Schedule: Parking lot open 4:00 a.m. to 10:00 p.m., when lot gate closes
Maps: USGS Del Mar OEW; trail map available online at www .californiacoastaltrail.info/hikers/ hikers_main.php?DisplayAction =DisplaySection&CountyId=21& SectionId=398
Trail contacts: Kellogg Park, 8200 Camino Del Oro, La Jolla, CA 92037; (619) 235-1169; www.san diego.gov/park-and-recreation/ parks/shoreline/kelloggpark.shtml
Special considerations: Alco-hol prohibited. Beach areas may become inaccessible during high tide.

Finding the trailhead: From I-5 north of I-8, exit onto La Jolla Parkway, then travel 1.1 miles until you come to the stoplight at the bottom of the hill. Turn right onto La Jolla Shores Drive and travel 0.3 mile before turning left onto Vallecitos. The parking lot will be on the right-hand side and fills up quickly. After parking, head to the beach and turn right (north). GPS: N32.857581 / W117.257413

THE HIKE

t's no surprise that the length of coast connecting two of the best beaches in San Diego County is one of the nicest walks. This 2.4-mile stretch connects La Jolla Shores Beach to Black's Beach in the north. La Jolla Shores is home to the Scripps Institution of Oceanography. The institute, often just called Scripps, is one of the largest ocean and earth science research centers in the world. It is the oldest oceanic research institute in the country, dating back to 1903. The institute was founded by contributions from early San Diego philanthropist Miss Ellen Scripps. During the early years, it was completely funded by Miss Scripps and her brother, E. W. Scripps. Eventually merging with the University of California system in 1912, the Scripps Institution of Oceanography became the point around which the University of California San Diego was founded in 1960. Scripps now boasts more than 100 faculty, 300 other scientists, and more than 200 graduate students, who work within the institution and operate the four oceanographic research vessels.

La Jolla Shores is one of the gentler beaches in the area, with few rip currents and smaller waves, although the ocean all along this hike is a popular for surfing. This also makes it a popular destination for beginning scuba classes and allows for one of the only beach boat-launch sites in the area. La Jolla Underwater Park Ecological Reserve borders the beach to the south, as does La Jolla Cove.

Scripps Pier is the crown jewel of the University of California's Scripps Institution of Oceanography.

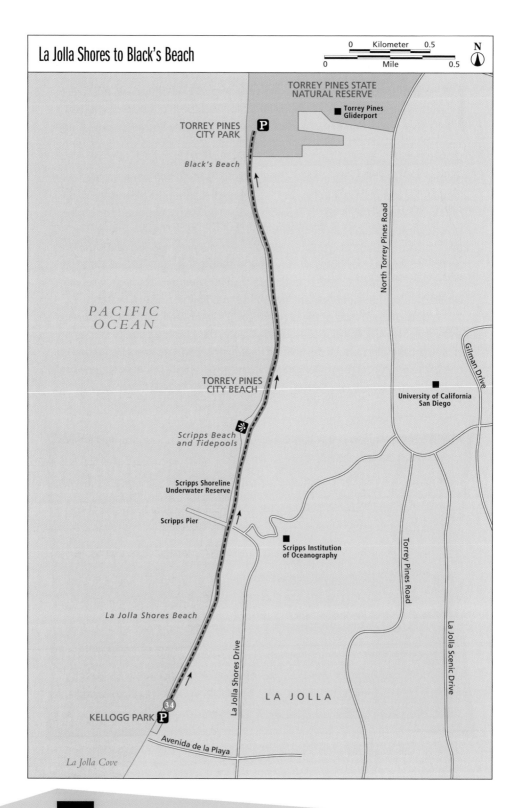

La Jolla Shores to Black's Beach

0   Kilometer   0.5
0   Mile   0.5

N

TORREY PINES STATE
NATURAL RESERVE

TORREY PINES
City Park

Torrey Pines
Gliderport

Black's Beach

North Torrey Pines Road

PACIFIC
OCEAN

Gilman Drive

TORREY PINES
CITY BEACH

University of California
San Diego

Scripps Beach
and Tidepools

Scripps Shoreline
Underwater Reserve

Scripps Pier

Scripps Institution
of Oceanography

Torrey Pines Road

La Jolla Shores Beach

La Jolla Shores Drive

LA JOLLA

La Jolla Scenic Drive

34

KELLOGG PARK

Avenida de la Playa

La Jolla Cove

Proceeding north from Kellogg Park, you will walk along one of the busiest local beaches in San Diego. Scripps Pier lies ahead; it is not open to the public but is a common spot for surfers and photographers. A little farther on there are rocks and tide pools that kids love to explore.

Leaving the crowds behind, scamper past the rocks to find a large, mushroom-shaped building. Is it a scientific research station? A missile silo? The lair of an evil genius? As this building is privately owned, no one knows for sure. Farther along the beach, people start to reappear, filtering in from the Salk Canyon access road. Black's Beach begins shortly after.

Black's Beach is a beautiful stretch of coast and perhaps the largest and most famous clothing-optional beach on the West Coast. Although never particularly crowded (all access points to the beach require some hiking), Black's is popular with surfers as well as nudists.

Go up the stairs to the sea cliffs at Torrey Pines Gliderport, which is a great place to end the hike if you have a ride. Otherwise, enjoy the clifftop view before returning the way you came.

MILES AND DIRECTIONS

0.0 Start at La Jolla Shores/Kellogg Park in La Jolla. Take to the beach and head north.

0.6 Pass Scripps Pier. This is a very popular spot for photographers around sunset.

0.7 The sand begins to recede, and the beach takes you along the high cliffs over rocks and tide pools.

1.0 Gawk at the strange building. Ponder its meaning before moving on.

2.2 Reach the stairs that lead up to Torrey Pines Gliderport. The hike up is fairly steep, but you *are* ascending a cliff.

2.4 Enjoy the bluff and all the colorful gliders before catching your ride. (**Option:** Head back down the beach for a 4.2-mile round-trip.)

Some people park at the gliderport above Black's Beach, but the unimproved paths carved by years of dedicated beachgoers are unstable and may be confusing. False trails have led many hikers to become stuck on the side of a cliff—or worse.

Manchester Reserve

One of Encinitas's newest reserves, this oasis in the middle of town offers a brisk hike with a chance of wildlife sightings. The reserve is embraced by houses on three sides, with the lagoon below. For a relatively small open space, the reserve offers the chance to get your legs burning up a steep hill, wildlife that includes endangered species, and a pretty impressive view. Not bad for the middle of town.

Start: The dirt parking lot before Trabert Ranch Road
Distance: 2.1-mile lollipop
Approximate hiking time: 1 hour
Difficulty: Easy to moderate
Trail surface: Dirt path
Best season: Fall, when birds are migrating
Other trail users: None
Canine compatibility: Leashed dogs allowed
Fees and permits: No fees or permits required
Schedule: Sunrise to sunset
Maps: USGS Encinitas; trail maps available online at www

.co.san-diego.ca.us/reusable _components/images/parks/ doc/Trails_OVRP.pdf, www .cityofencinitas.org/NR/ rdonlyres/416095A4-B85F-4D96-89E8-E64EFEA16659/0/ TrailmaintenanceMap5.pdf, and www.ci.encinitas.ca.us/NR/ rdonlyres/7A9526E7-0F4D-43D3-AD01-83EF13E0038D/0/park_ beach_fac_map.pdf
Trail contacts: Jessica S. Vinje, Preserve Manager (760-294-8439); Markus Spiegelberg, San Diego Area Manager (619-295-4953)

Finding the trailhead: From I-5 north take the Manchester Avenue exit, turning east. Follow the road and turn right, continuing on Manchester to follow the San Elijo Lagoon. (The road going straight is South El Camino Real.) About a mile after you leave the freeway, you'll see a large open space on your left and a dirt pull-off just before Trabert Ranch Road. Pull into the parking area. The sign for Manchester Reserve is beside the path heading up the mountain. GPS: N33.0287 / W117.2431

THE HIKE

The city of Encinitas offers 40 miles of trails throughout its city limits that permit only nonmotorized methods of transportation: feet, horse, or bike. While many of these trails feature watery venues, there are also options for those who prefer their walks high and dry. Perhaps because it is relatively unknown, the Manchester Mitigation Bank is surprisingly untrampled when you consider its proximity to houses and a college. (A mitigation bank is an area set aside by developers to mitigate the loss of native habitat caused by their projects.) In fact, it isn't unusual to be the only one on the trail, or at least within eyesight, as you hike the moderate hills.

In 1996 the nonprofit Center for Natural Lands Management (CNLM) took over the management of the area from a local developer, although the city maintains the actual trails. Throughout the state, CNLM manages 52,000 acres within seventy-two preserves, all of which harbor sensitive biological resources.

Manchester's 123-acre site lets you ascend from 40 to 275 feet above sea level—not a thigh-burning excursion but certainly enough to get your blood moving. As you climb you get high enough to see the city shimmering between the undeveloped foreground and the sea that sparkles against the horizon. You walk through coastal sage scrub, southern maritime chaparral, and a bit of willow woodland. The

Like the proverbial needle in a haystack, Manchester Reserve is a little-known sanctuary for those looking for nature in the bustling city of Encinitas.

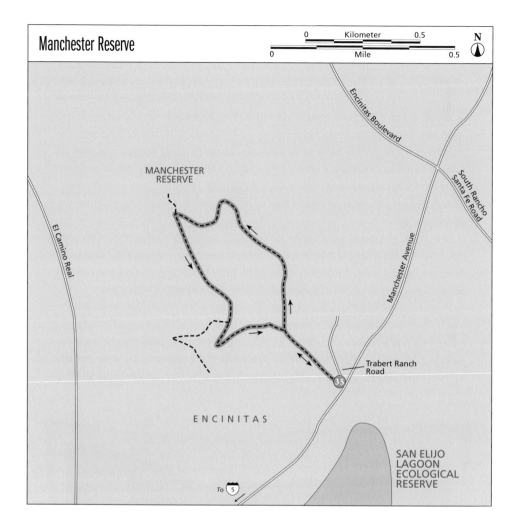

reserve hosts the endangered coastal California gnatcatcher as well as such endangered plants as the funnel-shaped San Diego thorn mint, Del Mar manzanita, and Orcutt's hazardia. Watch for the thorn mint's delicate violet flowers in spring and the bright-yellow blooms of the Orcutt's hazardia as summer turns into fall.

The hike begins just inside the dirt parking area on Manchester Avenue. A quick stop at the kiosk lets you know if there are any current restrictions or watches and provides an overview of the park trails. While there are several trail spurs, the whole area is pretty clearly defined by the houses that surround the perimeter.

The central trail follows an old power line road (probably the main reason the area remained undeveloped and retains most of its native habitat). Head up toward the peak for the best views and take advantage of the little trail spurs, avoiding any that head directly into someone's backyard (there are a few). The reserve urges hikers to stay on trails to protect the fragile remaining native habitat.

0.0 Start at the Manchester Reserve sign and head up the mountain.

0.1 Take the trail to the right to ascend to the steepest grade.

0.9 Take a 360-degree gander from the summit.

1.0 Keep heading north to catch a trail that heads back down.

1.5 Turn left to follow the wash that turns into a trail back down the slope. Then head back down the slope toward the car. (**Option:** You can see all the trail variations; take any spur that catches your fancy.)

2.1 Arrive back at the trailhead.

> *Volunteer Opportunity: Help maintain the trails and protect Manchester Reserve's fragile habitat. Contact the preserve manager for details: (760) 294-8439.*

Stairs on trails help prevent erosion.

Presidio Park—White Deer Trail

A secret hideaway in one of downtown's oldest parks leads you up to Inspiration Point, the site of one of San Diego's sweetest stories. While unknown to almost anyone beyond locals, the hike has an impressive list of attributes: great views, grassy hills, seasonal water, and an obscure yet touching bit of San Diego history.

Start: Parking lot on the north end of Taylor Street
Distance: 0.6-mile loop
Approximate hiking time: 30 minutes
Difficulty: Easy
Trail surface: Dirt path
Best season: Year-round
Other trail users: People with dogs, runners
Canine compatibility: Leashed dogs allowed
Fees and permits: No fees or permits required

Schedule: Park open 24 hours
Maps: USGS La Jolla; trail map available online at www.sandiego.gov/park-and-recreation/pdf/ppmap.pdf
Trail contacts: City of San Diego Park and Recreation Department, Developed Regional Parks Division, 2125 Park Blvd., San Diego CA 92101; (619) 235-1169

Finding the trailhead: From I-8, near the junction with I-5, exit onto Hotel Circle South. Cross the freeway onto the south side of I-8, turning west onto Taylor Street. Almost immediately on your left you'll see a small turnout with an open gate guard and a generous parking area. This is the entry to Presidio Park. With the restroom on your left, look up the canyon. The trail begins at the old service road, heading up the canyon wash. GPS: N32.759716 / W117.192780

THE HIKE

The ghost of the white deer still haunts Presidio Park. She flees from you as you hike up the trail, a glimpse of her white tail disappearing into the bushes. Sometimes she eats the flowers from local gardens, or her tracks can be seen on the early-morning mud. But there's no such thing as ghosts, so I'll tell you about the real Lucy.

Lucy was the name given to a white doe born in the San Diego Zoo in the late 1960s. While she may or may not have been sold to a private buyer in Mission Hills, all versions of the story include Lucy escaping from her place of residence into the sunset with a buck. Lucy wandered Mission Valley, Mission Hills, and Presidio Park for about ten years, becoming a fixture while her male companion was never heard from again. Local residents became enamored. They fed Lucy, watched her, and adopted her as part of the community.

Then tragedy struck. In the early morning hours one crisp day, residents frantically began calling the local police. Lucy was trying to cross the busy I-8 freeway, and she was in danger of being hit. After a quick assessment, police called in animal control to save the frantic creature.

Try as they might, the animal control officers were unable to capture poor, terrified Lucy. In desperation, and with her supporters in a near frenzy, they loaded up

Despite its central location, Presidio Park can feel wild and remote.

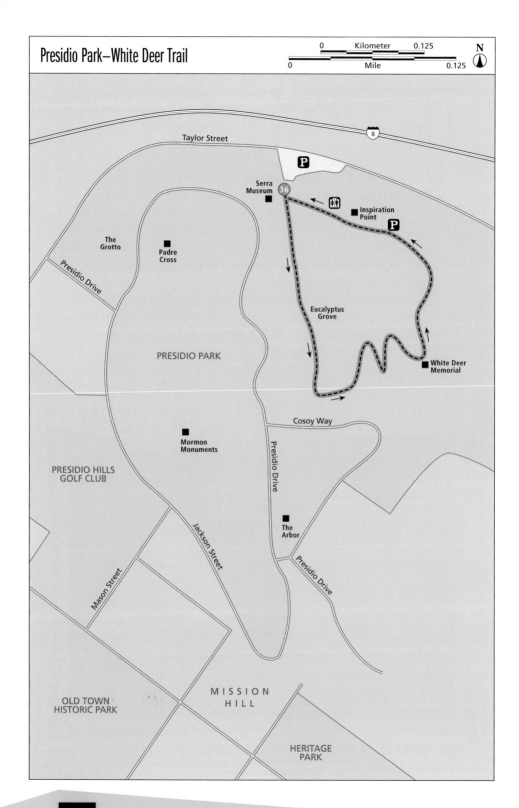

Presidio Park–White Deer Trail

Taylor Street

Serra Museum

Inspiration Point

The Grotto

Padre Cross

Eucalyptus Grove

PRESIDIO PARK

White Deer Memorial

Cosoy Way

Presidio Drive

Mormon Monuments

PRESIDIO HILLS GOLF CLUB

Jackson Street

Mason Street

The Arbor

Presidio Drive

OLD TOWN HISTORIC PARK

MISSION HILL

HERITAGE PARK

0   Kilometer   0.125

0   Mile   0.125

N

the tranquilizer gun. As the dart zipped through the air, the officer had no way of knowing that the cold steel tip of a hypodermic needle would be the last thing the majestic white deer would ever feel.

The tranquilizer worked too well. Lucy's breath became labored. Slowed. Stopped.

The community mourned the loss of its friend and organized a memorial service at Inspiration Point that was attended by more than 200 people. Lucy was laid to rest on the hill she was so fond of, and residents pooled funds to construct a memorial in her honor.

They installed three native stones beside a shallow water basin that would permanently offer refreshment to other wild creatures. A small bronze plaque is inscribed with the following words: "THE WHITE DEER OF MISSION HILLS: BLISS IN SOLITUDE BENEATH THIS TREE. FORMLESS, SILENT, SPIRIT FREE. ~ A FRIEND."

The hike begins at the parking lot off Taylor Street and heads up the canyon, following the wash. You can see a winding path that leads up to the museum and the main section of the park. The park is quiet, with tall eucalyptus trees and large expanses of grassy areas. You will wind your way up the opposite hill, heading left.

The short hike takes you to the top of Inspiration Point, which provides a lovely view over the San Diego River Valley. Look for the memorial plaque tucked away in a secluded corner. Take a moment to reflect on the fleeting nature of fragile things before moving back down the right side of the hill and returning to your car.

MILES AND DIRECTIONS

0.0 Start at the parking lot on the north end of Taylor Street and head straight into Palm Canyon.

0.1 As the canyon abuts private property, stick to the left and proceed up the path that leads up the side of the canyon.

0.2 Reach the top of the canyon among a grove of pine trees. Stay to the right as you walk up the grassy hill.

0.3 Arrive at the White Deer Memorial at the top right corner of the hill.

0.4 Keeping to the highway side of the hill going down, you'll pass through a parking lot. The trail continues directly across on the far west side and heads down to the trailhead.

0.6 Arrive back at the parking lot.

San Elijo Reserve Nature Center Trail

This short, easy trail takes you through key ecological areas within the reserve for views of nesting waterbirds, grassy marshlands, and quiet woods. The tour begins at the LEED Award–winning visitor center and then moves to a boardwalk featuring the lagoon with the sea as a backdrop. Perfect for hikers with children or those with limited ability, this trail allows all visitors the chance to get out in nature.

Start: San Elijo Reserve Nature Center on Manchester Avenue

Distance: 0.5-mile loop

Approximate hiking time: 30 minutes

Difficulty: Easy

Trail surface: Boardwalk, dirt path

Best season: April through May and August through October, when the annual bird migration is at its peak

Other trail users: Naturalists, critters

Canine compatibility: No dogs allowed

Fees and permits: No fees or permits required

Schedule: Reserve open during daylight hours only; visitor center open 9:00 a.m. to 5:00 p.m. daily except Christmas Day

Maps: USGS Encinitas; trail map available online at www.co.san-diego.ca.us/reusable_components/images/parks/doc/Trails_San_Elijo.pdf

Trail contacts: San Elijo Lagoon Ecological Reserve, 2710 Manchester Ave., Cardiff-by-the-Sea, CA 92007; (760) 634 3026; www.co.san-diego.ca.us/parks/open space/selr.html

Special considerations: The reserve offers free guided nature walks that start from the nature center on Saturday morning at 10:00 a.m. Every second Monday, the center organizes bird counts. Call (760) 436-3944 for details. Every third Saturday, volunteers gather to clean up the lagoon.

Finding the trailhead: From I-5 just north of Solana Beach, take the Manchester Avenue exit and turn west, going under the freeway. After the freeway, the nature center is the first driveway on your left. GPS: N33.0134 / W117.2742

THE HIKE

San Elijo Lagoon Ecological Reserve is one of the best-kept secrets in North County. It offers 7 miles of hiking trails within 1,000 acres of freshwater wetlands, salt marsh, coastal strand, riparian scrub, coastal sage scrub, and mixed chaparral. The diverse plant communities attract a wealth of wildlife, particularly birds. Birders come from all over the world to observe the wide variety of species within the 77-square-mile watershed drained by its two creeks.

More than 300 species of birds live or migrate through the reserve. Over a third of the migrating species are rare or uncommon; another seventy-four species are considered sensitive, threatened, or endangered. Of the sixty-five species of nesting birds, seventeen are sensitive, threatened, or endangered.

Literally thousands of birds call the lagoon and coast home, or at least their vacation home. During your hike, look for the federally endangered brown pelican and light-footed clapper rail; least terns nest closer to the coast. Inland, watch for least Bell's vireos along Escondido Creek, federally threatened snowy plovers, California gnatcatchers, and state-endangered Belding's savannah sparrows. Hawks and eagles are often sighted, including the recently delisted peregrine falcon as a regular visitor.

The hike begins at the nature center and heads out to the saltwater marsh. Along the muddy banks watch for shorebirds nesting and digging for food. To the

The San Elijo Reserve Nature Center offers access to a surprisingly wild ecosystem.

San Elijo Reserve Nature Center Trail

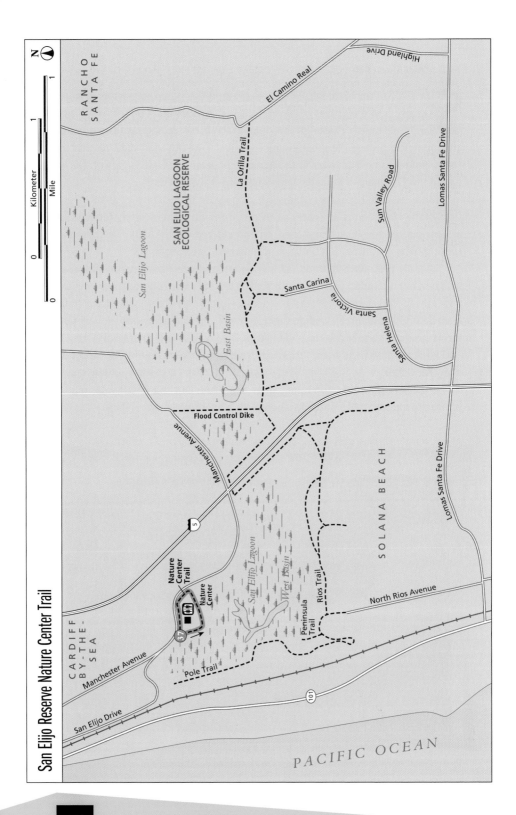

west, the railroad can be seen in the distance, as well as a glimpse of the ocean. Salty Susan, salty dodder, salt grass, and pickle weed flourish in the west and central basins. In the past, the mouth of the lagoon became filled with sediment, but with the lagoon now under protection, the natural ebb and flow between the lagoon and the sea have reinvigorated the salt marsh.

Three-quarters of the way through the hike you'll reach a small stand of lush riparian scrub that depends on seasonal rains flooding the area, then seasonal sun drying it out again. It isn't uncommon to find mulefat, miner's lettuce, willow, and eucalyptus growing in these areas. Stand still for a few minutes and you might encounter a local inhabitant, as curious about you as you are about it. Keep going and you'll get back to the parking area.

MILES AND DIRECTIONS

0.0   Start at the trailhead northwest of the nature center and bear right to follow the loop.

0.1   The trail features various lookouts and benches. Stop at the first kiosk and read. Follow the path around, stopping to look for birds and read the informational plaques.

0.4   Wander under a canopy of branches. Continue along the boardwalk.

0.5   Reach the end of the boardwalk and return to the parking lot.

Being "Greenest"

In 2009 the San Elijo Reserve Nature Center was recognized as San Diego County's "greenest" public building with a LEED Platinum Certification. The 5,600-square-foot center won its award from its use of photovoltaic solar panels that provide more than half the center's energy needs; its use of renewable lumber in construction; and the use of radiant floors, natural lighting, and natural ventilation to reduce energy consumption.

Silver Strand Stretch

Hike this slim spit of land between the crashing waves of the Pacific Ocean and the silvery blue waters of San Diego Bay. The hike takes you beachside alongside fenced-off military property south of the state park that segregates the public from the coastal dunes. Because this stretch is accessible only to those hearty enough to hike the distance, the pristine beach shows what the coast would be like if it were human free.

Start: Southernmost end of the parking lot at Silver Strand State Beach

Distance: 3.3 miles point to point

Approximate hiking time: 1.5 hours

Difficulty: Easy

Trail surface: Sand

Best season: Year-round

Other trail users: Beachcombers, runners, romantics, and shorebirds

Canine compatibility: Leashed dogs allowed only in the day-use and camping area parking lots

Fees and permits: Parking fee for Silver Strand State Beach

Schedule: Front gate open year-round 8:00 a.m. to 7:00 p.m.

Maps: USGS Point Loma; trail maps available online at www .californiacoastaltrail.info/hikers/ hikers_main.php?DisplayAction =DisplaySection&CountyId=21& SectionId=409 and www.california coastaltrail.info/hikers/hikers _main.php?DisplayAction=Display Section&CountyId=21&Section Id=407

Trail contacts: Silver Strand State Beach, 5000 Hwy. 75, Coronado, CA 92118; (619) 522-7300 or (619) 435-5184

City of Coronado, 1825 Strand Way, Coronado, CA 92118; (619) 522-7300

Finding the trailhead: From I-5 south cross over the Coronado Bay Bridge into Coronado. Continue until you meet Orange Avenue, onto which you'll turn left. Orange Avenue soon turns into CA 75, which runs directly through the strand, separating the beach from the bay. Silver Strand State Beach is located about 4.5 miles south of the city of Coronado. The trail begins at the southernmost end of the state beach parking lot. GPS: N32.6822 / W117.1807

THE HIKE

The Silver Strand has always been one of the most magical stretches of beach in Southern California. It is still possible, although increasingly rare, to find sand dollars and angel wings in the sand here. If the sand dollars are purple or green, throw them back into the sea—they are still alive. However, if they are white, the animal once inside has probably been eaten. Look for a hole in the shell where the flesh has been sucked out. The once-common angel wing shells form a translucent silvery-white "wing" that gave the strand its name and made beach-combing particularly engrossing. Because this is a state beach, all shells, plants, and animals are protected and may not be removed.

Coronado is not actually an island. This slim stretch of land connects it to Imperial Beach, which is part of the mainland. The strand was first developed when a road was scraped through the center to make way for future homebuyers. A steam train was quickly added to help connect the Coronado Hotel with the mainland, bringing in passengers and supplies and exporting the garbage to local hog and chicken farms on the mainland.

But when J. D. and A. B. Spreckels Investment Co. bought the Coronado Beach Company after the 1888 market crash, development was given a second thought. The holding company donated the land to the state in 1931. The U.S. Navy took

White sands that seem to stretch forever are the hallmark of the Silver Strand.

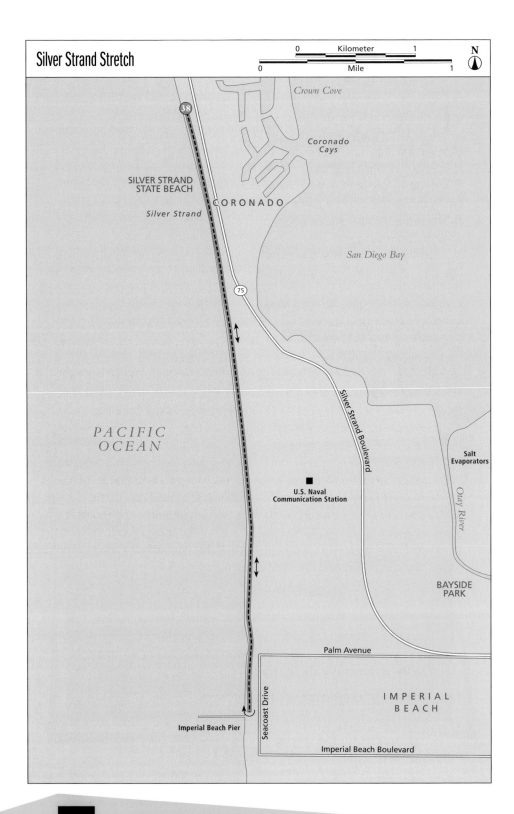

Silver Strand Stretch

0   Kilometer   1

0   Mile   1

N

Crown Cove

Coronado Cays

SILVER STRAND STATE BEACH

CORONADO

Silver Strand

San Diego Bay

PACIFIC OCEAN

Silver Strand Boulevard

Salt Evaporators

Otay River

U.S. Naval Communication Station

BAYSIDE PARK

Palm Avenue

Seacoast Drive

IMPERIAL BEACH

Imperial Beach Pier

Imperial Beach Boulevard

over some parcels in 1941 and dredged much of their holdings. The good news was that they dumped the discarded sand along the strand, raising it above its position as little more than a mudflat and expanding the beach from a 40-foot strip to the beach you see today.

By 1955 the California Department of Parks and Recreation had gained complete control of the "artificially accreted lands and tide and submerged lands." The Navy still retains the parcels they acquired during World War II. The strand, both the ocean and the bay sides, fosters some of the most critical wildlife and nesting habitats of the coastal California wetlands. You can continue beneath the underpass to access the bayside estuary, where you can often find egrets, bitterns, herons, godwits, and sandpipers.

The hike begins at the southern end of the state park and continues alongside a fenced-off, restricted area that keeps the traffic low on the beach side. Sandy dunes host a nesting area for the threatened western snowy plover. These small, inauspicious shorebirds are a delight to watch. The flock cautiously sends a scout to check out the site before the rest land, where they will neatly pick off flies from discarded sea kelp. You'll see some of the best coastal dunes left in Southern California, as well as easy waves that wash up kelp and small shells.

As you near restricted military areas, try not to peer obviously into their territory—frankly, there is little to see. We've never been able to find out what they do there, but there are weird shapes, electrical things, and mysterious activities. This is San Diego's Area 51, and it does keep the crowds away. Access is restricted, but you may continue to walk along the beach.

During winter it is possible to see California gray whales on their annual calving migration. Just at the end of the restricted area, a long, rocky jetty kicks into the sea. A little while later, a second jetty parallels the first. It is unclear why the jetties are here, as this is neither a port nor the mouth of a river. However, kayakers and anglers like them. A little farther on, the Imperial Beach Fishing Pier reaches into the sea and offers great views and good snacks. Pick up your ride at the base of the pier, or turn around and walk back to the parking lot.

MILES AND DIRECTIONS

0.0   Start at the southern end of the Silver Strand State Beach parking lot. If you don't want to pay the fee, there is free street-side parking across the street (via the underpass) at the Coronado Cays.

1.4   A military something borders the sand dunes.

2.7   A stone jetty, function unknown, extends into the sea. You should be able to go around it on the land side at most times; if you cannot get around it, crawl over.

2.75   The military base ends and Imperial Beach begins.

2.8   Come to another jetty.

3.3   Take a walk on Imperial Beach Pier before meeting your ride. (**Option:** Walk back to your car for a 6.6-mile round-trip hike.)

Nature Walk

Join fellow wildlife enthusiasts on Sunday from 1:30 to 2:30 p.m. for an hour-long guided walk that explores the plant and animal wildlife along Silver Strand State Beach. Participants meet outside the lifeguard headquarters at the tall tower on the ocean side of the highway. Rangers recommend bringing binoculars and hand lenses. This is a breeding area for the western snowy plover as well as home to the famous local grunion runs.

The park has partnered with Loews Resort to enlist volunteers to participate in restoring critical breeding and nesting habitat. Call (619) 424-4000 and ask for the Loews Resort concierge to find out more about the program, or call (619) 823-5801 to volunteer to be part of the Plover Patrol.

As of this printing, the State of California and City of San Diego were experiencing severe budget cuts. Hours of operation, lifeguard hours, and other services may not be what they were when this research was conducted. Please call ahead to confirm services before heading out.

Tijuana Estuary—North McCoy Trail

One of the major drainage deltas in Southern California, the Tijuana Estuary serves as one of the most important and vibrant ecosystems in San Diego County. A haven for birders, these wetlands teem with life in the mornings and evenings. This hike is perfect for people whose prime focus is observing the natural world.

Start: Visitor center or trailhead on the left side of the parking lot

Distance: 0.8 mile out and back

Approximate hiking time: 30 minutes

Difficulty: Easy

Trail surface: Dirt path

Best season: Fall and spring, when bird migration is in full swing

Other trail users: None

Canine compatibility: No dogs allowed

Fees and permits: No fees or permits required

Schedule: Trails open sunrise to sunset; visitor center open Wed through Sun 10:00 a.m. to 5:00 p.m.

Maps: USGS Imperial Beach; trail map available online at http://trnerr.org/site/?page_id=577

Trail contacts: Tijuana River National Estuarine Research Reserve, 301 Caspian Way, Imperial Beach, CA 91932; (619) 575-3613; http://trnerr.org/site/
    Tijuana Slough National Wildlife Refuge; (619) 575-2704; www.fws.gov/refuges/profiles/index.cfm?id=81681

Special considerations: Many guided hikes and education and volunteer opportunities are available. Don't forget your binoculars. No digging or collecting of shells, rocks, wood, plants, or animals is permitted.

Other: Equestrian trails are available on the south end of the Tijuana Estuary in Border Field State Park.

Finding the trailhead: Take I-5 south to exit 4 (Coronado Avenue) toward Imperial Beach. Turn right and continue along Coronado Avenue for about 2.5 miles. Coronado Avenue becomes Imperial Beach Boulevard at 13th Street; turn left onto Third Street and take a quick left again onto Caspian Way, which will take you straight into the parking lot (free parking). The trailhead begins just to the left side of the parking lot; you can also begin your hike from the visitor center. GPS: N32.344909 / W117.74304

THE HIKE

For a hiker, it's easy to fall into the habit of moving as fast as the body is willing. To feel the body stretch and strain against the world's curves is one of the great joys of hiking and is what draws so many to the sport again and again. Yet there are other reasons to be outside that are sometimes lost to that fast-moving mentality. The Tijuana Slough is the perfect place to remind yourself that sometimes just being outdoors is the point.

Of the more than 370 species of bird that reside in the Tijuana Slough throughout the year, seven are considered endangered or threatened. Benches and lookouts are common throughout the reserve and are some of the best places for catching a glimpse of one of them. Bitterns and herons can often be seen wading in the shallow wetlands as they stalk small fish and shellfish. These birds will wait for hours at a time in their hunt for food. You need not be as patient, but waiting until they find something can be equally rewarding for you.

The rare and complex ecosystem is the subject of ongoing research within the reserve. Many colleges, universities, and professional researchers use the reserve to study wetlands. Ninety percent of Southern California's coastal wetlands have already been destroyed to make way for development. The thirty years of research done in the Tijuana Estuary Reserve has been critical to developing effective wetlands management to protect environmental resources both here and around

The relatively short North McCoy Trail leads you into a quiet slough.

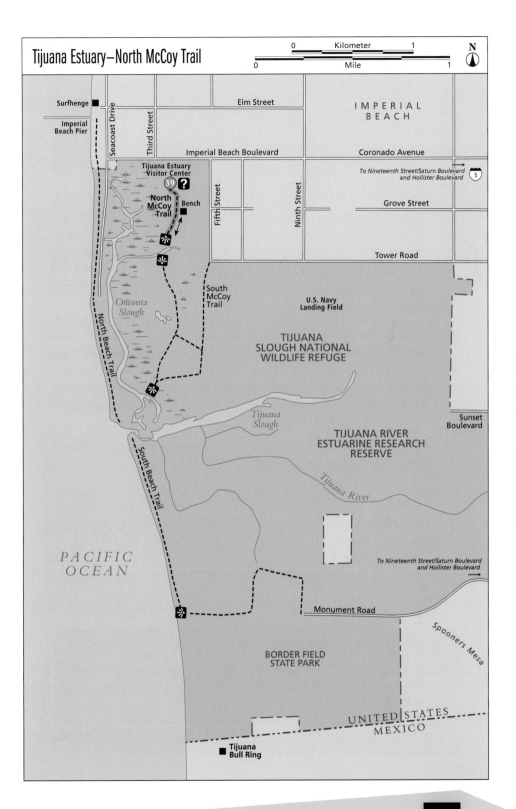

Tijuana Estuary–North McCoy Trail

0 Kilometer 1

0 Mile 1

N

Surfhenge

Imperial Beach Pier

Seacoast Drive

Third Street

Elm Street

IMPERIAL
BEACH

Imperial Beach Boulevard

Coronado Avenue

Tijuana Estuary
Visitor Center

39 ?

North
McCoy
Trail

Bench

Fifth Street

Ninth Street

To Nineteenth Street/Saturn Boulevard
and Hollister Boulevard

5

Grove Street

South
McCoy
Trail

U.S. Navy
Landing Field

Tower Road

Oneonta
Slough

North Beach Trail

TIJUANA
SLOUGH NATIONAL
WILDLIFE REFUGE

Tijuana
Slough

Sunset
Boulevard

South Beach Trail

TIJUANA RIVER
ESTUARINE RESEARCH
RESERVE

Tijuana River

PACIFIC
OCEAN

To Nineteenth Street/Saturn Boulevard
and Hollister Boulevard

Monument Road

Spooners Mesa

BORDER FIELD
STATE PARK

UNITED STATES
MEXICO

Tijuana
Bull Ring

the country. Volunteers run an educational water quality monitoring laboratory to study contamination of the estuary waters. Water conditions are also carefully monitored every half hour at multiple sites around the reserve.

Business aside, Tijuana Estuary is one of the best-kept secrets in the county. Its serenity lies in stark contrast to the crowded beaches located less than a mile away. Hawks circle and soar as Navy helicopters come and go. The secrets of the slough are slowly revealed as you simply watch and wait. The birds, the plants, and the river will all take you in if you can simply slow down to their pace.

MILES AND DIRECTIONS

0.0 Start at the parking lot of the Tijuana Estuary Visitor Center. Make your way through the front entrance, where you'll find a large map of the Tijuana watershed. Inside are a variety of excellent exhibits discussing the ecosystems located within the marsh.

0.1 Continue out the south entrance of the building (to your left as you walk in the front entrance). From here you will hit a network of small, interconnected trails. How you proceed is not so important. As long as you keep going generally south and east (straight and to your left) into the estuary, you will soon hit the North McCoy Trail, the slightly wider path going into the wetlands and away from the houses. Turn right onto the trail.

0.2 Come to a bench to your left. This is a good place to bird-watch. (You did bring your binoculars, didn't you?)

0.4 Reach the end of the hike, where you will find another bench and a fantastic view. (FYI: Across the river you can see another lookout on the South McCoy Trail, which cannot be accessed from this point.) Return the way you came. (**Option:** Stay awhile and watch the birds. Sunset is a wonderful time to be in the estuary.)

0.8 Arrive back at the trailhead.

The Tijuana River National Estuarine Research Reserve hosts free lectures that present information on the ongoing research within the reserve. Call (619) 575-3614 for upcoming lectures. The visitor center also schedules regular weekend nature and bird walks led by expert docents.

Tijuana Estuary—South McCoy Trail

The south side of the Tijuana River National Estuarine Research Reserve offers more in both hiking trail length and diversity than other parts of the delta. Great views of San Diego's sister city, Tijuana, can be had throughout the hike. This section of the reserve allows bikes but also offers plenty of privacy, as well as a number of benches where you can sit silently with your binoculars and watch the birds and other wildlife emerge.

Start: Trailhead on the estuary side of the parking lot

Distance: 2.8 miles out and back

Approximate hiking time: 2 hours

Difficulty: Easy

Trail surface: Dirt path

Best season: Fall and spring, when bird migration is in full swing

Other trail users: Cyclists

Canine compatibility: Leashed dogs allowed

Fees and permits: No fees or permits required

Schedule: Trails open sunrise to sunset; visitor center open Wed through Sun from 10:00 a.m. to 5:00 p.m.

Maps: USGS Imperial Beach; trail map available online at http://trnerr.org/site/?page_id=577

Trail contacts: Tijuana River National Estuarine Research Reserve, 301 Caspian Way, Imperial Beach, CA 91932; (619) 575-3613; http://trnerr.org/site/
Tijuana Slough National Wildlife Refuge; (619) 575-2704; www.fws.gov/refuges/profiles/index.cfm?id=81681

Special considerations: Many guided hikes and education and volunteer opportunities are available. Don't forget your binoculars. No digging or collecting of shells, rocks, wood, plants, or animals is permitted.

Other: Equestrian trails are available on the south end of the Tijuana Estuary in Border Field State Park.

Finding the trailhead: Take I-5 south to exit 4 (Coronado Avenue) toward Imperial Beach. Turn right and continue along Coronado Avenue for about 2.4 miles. Coronado Avenue becomes Imperial Beach Boulevard at 13th Street; turn left onto Fifth Street after 8 blocks. Shortly after, Fifth Street dead-ends at the U.S. Navy airfield and Iris Street. A small parking lot is to the right, directly by a fence. The trailhead begins on the estuary side of the parking lot. GPS: N32.5693 / W117.1227

THE HIKE

San Diego is known for having a diverse variety of microclimates. Nowhere is this more apparent than in the Tijuana Estuary. A few inches in elevation, a slight difference in soil composition or salinity, can create vastly different features. Brackish pond, coastal sage scrub, dune, mudflat, salt panne, salt marsh, riparian, vernal pool—all these habitats exist in the Tijuana Estuary, and you'll be able to see most of them within the bounds of this hike.

Unique species of plants and animals live in each of these microhabitats, and many, such as mudflats and salt pannes, exist only in these wetland areas. Salt pannes are a unique environment that forms only in brackish waters when pools become isolated during the dryer months. Water evaporates, leaving a higher salinity than the source water that can increase from season to season. A variety of rare grasses thrive only in these salty conditions.

As the Tijuana River dries up during the summer, the flow of fresh water to the estuary is diminished, leaving more dry ground and shallower water. These things all contribute to the complexity of the California coastal wetlands and are why they're so critical and extraordinary.

Over the decades in which the estuary has been observed, numerous species of birds have come and gone from the area as the environment changed. Conditions have evolved to the point that the status of many species is currently unknown. More than 370 species of birds have been recorded in Tijuana Estuary, although many of those birds no longer exist here. This diversity has caused the American Bird Conservancy to recognize the reserve as a Globally Important Bird Area.

MILES AND DIRECTIONS

0.0   Start at the parking lot on the corner of Fifth Street and Iris Avenue. Proceed into the estuary and head left down the dirt path, along the U.S. Navy landing field.

0.3   Keep straight at the junction, where a trail heads off to your right. This will be your return route.

0.7   The trail makes a sharp right, away from the airstrip.

1.0   Continue straight, past the trail leading right.

1.2   The trail splits in a perfect T. Follow the left path a short distance to reach a great lookout. Double back to the intersection and take the north path.

1.5   Keep left past the fork.

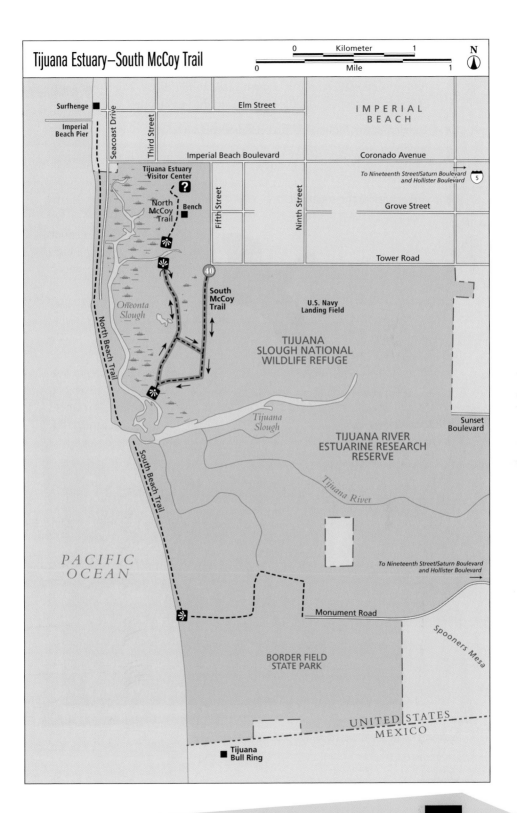

Tijuana Estuary–South McCoy Trail

0 Kilometer 1
0 Mile 1

N

Surfhenge

Imperial Beach Pier

Seacoast Drive

Third Street

Elm Street

IMPERIAL BEACH

Imperial Beach Boulevard

Coronado Avenue

To Nineteenth Street/Saturn Boulevard and Hollister Boulevard

5

Tijuana Estuary Visitor Center

North McCoy Trail

Bench

Fifth Street

Ninth Street

Grove Street

Tower Road

40

South McCoy Trail

U.S. Navy Landing Field

Oneonta Slough

TIJUANA SLOUGH NATIONAL WILDLIFE REFUGE

North Beach Trail

Sunset Boulevard

Tijuana Slough

TIJUANA RIVER ESTUARINE RESEARCH RESERVE

South Beach Trail

Tijuana River

PACIFIC OCEAN

To Nineteenth Street/Saturn Boulevard and Hollister Boulevard

Monument Road

Spooners Mesa

BORDER FIELD STATE PARK

UNITED STATES
MEXICO

Tijuana Bull Ring

2.0 Arrive at the final lookout point. You can see one of the streams that run through the estuary; this is a great place to find birds. When you finish enjoying the scenery, double back toward the last junction.

2.4 Turn left at the T junction. This time proceed left (east).

2.5 Come to the airfield. Head left at the junction to get back to the starting point.

2.8 Arrive back at the trailhead.

Subtle and mysterious flowers bloom along the South McCoy Trail.

Appendix: Clubs and Trail Groups

American Volkssport Association
www.ava.org/gen3/data/clubsbystate.asp?EVState=CA
This affiliate of the international walking group organizes historical, cultural, and scenic hikes in the San Diego area. The organization has a number of clubs throughout San Diego County. Check the website for the one closest to where you live or want to walk.

San Diego Audubon Society
4010 Morena Blvd., Suite 100
San Diego, CA 92117
(858) 273-7800
Affiliated with the national birding organization, this group provides information on birding areas and organizes birding hikes.

San Diego Chapter of the Sierra Club
8304 Clairemont Mesa Blvd. #101
San Diego, CA 92111
(858) 569-600
http://sandiego.sierraclub.org/home/index.asp
The regional chapter of the country's oldest, largest, and most influential environmental organization offers a wide array of opportunities to get out, help preserve the area, and advocate for a greener world.

San Diego Hiking Club
www.sandiegohikingclub.org/
Founded in 1980 by the late Skip Ruland and part of the Wilderness Association of San Diego, Inc., this group meets regularly for hikes, overnight camping, and to preserve the county's native beauty.

Coastwalk California
825 Gravenstein Hwy. North #8
Sebastopol, CA 95472
(707) 829-6689 or (800) 550-6854
www.coastwalk.org
This volunteer organization advocates for completion of the California Coastal Trail, making the California coast and beaches accessible to everyone. For more information on the trail, visit www.californiacoastaltrail.info/cms/pages/main/index.html.

The Nature Conservancy
San Diego Office
402 West Broadway, Suite 1350
San Diego, CA 92101
(619) 209-5830
www.nature.org/wherewework/northamerica/states/california/preserves/
art9761.html
The Nature Conservancy is very active in California and in San Diego County in particular, helping to protect and restore coastal wetlands, inland grasslands, and everything in between.

San Diego County Wildlife Federation (SDCWF)
P.O. Box 607
Solana Beach, CA 92075
(619) 226-1164
This chapter of the national organization supports the acquisition, restoration, development, and maintenance of wildlands and natural resources, particularly in relation to horseback riding; hiking; hunting; angling; shooting sports; falconry; the training, testing, and trailing of hunting dogs; and other related outdoor activities.

San Diego Native Plant Society
California Native Plant Society, San Diego Chapter
c/o San Diego Natural History Museum
P.O. Box 121390
San Diego, CA 92112-1390
www.cnpssd.org
E-mail: info@cnpssd.org
This is a local chapter of a statewide group promoting "understanding and appreciation of California's native plants." They work to preserve natural habitat through science, education, conservation, and restoration.

Friends of Cardiff & Carlsbad State Beaches
www.fccsb.org
Facebook: Friends of Cardiff and Carlsbad State Beaches (FCCSB)

Southwest Wetlands Interpretive Association (SWIA)
P.O. Box 575
Imperial Beach, CA 91933
(619) 575-0550
Founded in 1979, SWIA is dedicated to education about and acquisition, preservation, and restoration of wetlands.

The Art of Hiking

When standing nose to nose with a mountain lion, you're probably not too concerned with the issue of ethical behavior in the wild. No doubt you're just terrified. But let's be honest. How often are you nose to nose with a mountain lion? For most of us, a hike into the "wild" means loading up the SUV with expensive gear and driving to a toileted trailhead. Sure, you can mourn how civilized we've become—how GPS units have replaced natural instinct and Gore-Tex stands in for true-grit—but the silly gadgets of civilization aside, we have plenty of reason to take pride in how we've matured. With survival now on the back burner, we've begun to understand that we have a responsibility to protect, no longer just conquer, our wild places: that they, not we, are at risk. The following section will help you understand better what it means to "do what you can" while still making the most of your hiking experience. Anyone can take a hike, but hiking safely and well is an art requiring preparation and proper equipment.

Trail Etiquette

Leave no trace. Always leave an area just like you found it—if not better than you found it. Avoid camping in fragile, alpine meadows and along the banks of streams and lakes. Use a camp stove versus building a wood fire. Pack up all of your trash and extra food. Bury human waste at least 100 feet from water sources under 6 to 8 inches of topsoil. Don't bathe with soap in a lake or stream—use prepackaged moistened towels to wipe off sweat and dirt, or bathe in the water without soap.

Stay on the trail. It's true, a path anywhere leads nowhere new, but purists will just have to get over it. Paths serve an important purpose; they limit impact on natural areas. Straying from a designated trail may seem innocent but it can cause damage to sensitive areas—damage that may take years to recover, if it can recover at all. Even simple shortcuts can be destructive. So, please, stay on the trail.

Leave no weeds. Noxious weeds tend to overtake other plants, which in turn affects animals and birds that depend on them for food. To minimize the spread of noxious weeds, hikers should regularly clean their boots, tents, packs, and hiking poles of mud and seeds. Also brush your dog to remove any weed seeds before heading off into a new area.

Keep your dog under control. You can buy a flexi-lead that allows your dog to go exploring along the trail, while allowing you the ability to reel him in should another hiker approach or should he decide to chase a rabbit. Always obey leash laws and be sure to bury your dog's waste or pack it in resealable plastic bags.

Respect other trail users. Often you're not the only one on the trail. With the rise in popularity of multiuse trails, you'll have to learn a new kind of respect, beyond the nod and "hello" approach you may be used to. First investigate whether you're on a multiuse trail, and assume the appropriate precautions. When you encounter motorized vehicles (ATVs, motorcycles, and 4WDs), be alert. Though they should always yield to the hiker, often they're going too fast or are too lost in the buzz of their engine to react to your presence. If you hear activity ahead, step off the trail just to be safe. Note that you're not likely to hear a mountain biker coming, so be prepared and know ahead of time whether you share the trail with them. Cyclists should always yield to hikers, but that's little comfort to the hiker. Be aware.

When you approach horses or pack animals on the trail, always step quietly off the trail, preferably on the downhill side, and let them pass. If you're wearing a large backpack, it's often a good idea to sit down. To some animals, a hiker wearing a large backpack might appear threatening. Many national forests allow domesticated grazing, usually for sheep and cattle. Make sure your dog doesn't harass these animals, and respect ranchers' rights while you're enjoying yours.

Getting into Shape
Unless you want to be sore—and possibly have to shorten your trip or vacation—be sure to get in shape before a big hike. If you're terribly out of shape, start a walking program early, preferably eight weeks in advance. Start with a fifteen-minute walk during your lunch hour or after work and gradually increase your walking time to an hour. You should also increase your elevation gain. Walking briskly up hills really strengthens your leg muscles and gets your heart rate up. If you work in a storied office building, take the stairs instead of the elevator. If you prefer going to a gym, walk the treadmill or use a stair machine. You can further increase your strength and endurance by walking with a loaded backpack. Stationary exercises you might consider are squats, leg lifts, sit-ups, and push-ups. Other good ways to get in shape include biking, running, aerobics, and, of course, short hikes. Stretching before and after a hike keeps muscles flexible and helps avoid injuries.

Preparedness
It's been said that failing to plan means planning to fail. So do take the necessary time to plan your trip. Whether going on a short day hike or an extended backpack trip, always prepare for the worst. Simply remembering to pack a copy of the U.S. Army Survival Manual is not preparedness. Although it's not a bad idea if you plan on entering truly wild places, it's merely the tourniquet answer to a problem. You need to do your best to prevent the problem from arising in the first place. In order to survive—and to stay reasonably comfortable—you need to concern yourself with the basics: water, food, and shelter. Don't go on a hike without having these bases covered. And don't go on a hike expecting to find these items in the woods.

Water. Even in frigid conditions, you need at least two quarts of water a day to function efficiently. Add heat and taxing terrain and you can bump that figure up to one gallon. That's simply a base to work from—your metabolism and your level of conditioning can raise or lower that amount. Unless you know your level, assume that you need one gallon of water a day. Now, where do you plan on getting the water?

Preferably not from natural water sources. These sources can be loaded with intestinal disturbers, such as bacteria, viruses, and fertilizers. *Giardia lamblia,* the most common of these disturbers, is a protozoan parasite that lives part of its life cycle as a cyst in water sources. The parasite spreads when mammals defecate in water sources. Once ingested, Giardia can induce cramping, diarrhea, vomiting, and fatigue within two days to two weeks after ingestion. Giardiasis is treatable with prescription drugs. If you believe you've contracted giardiasis, see a doctor immediately.

Treating water. The best and easiest solution to avoid polluted water is to carry your water with you. Yet, depending on the nature of your hike and the duration, this may not be an option—one gallon of water weighs eight-and-a-half pounds. In that case, you'll need to look into treating water. Regardless of which method you choose, you should always carry some water with you in case of an emergency. Save this reserve until you absolutely need it.

There are three methods of treating water: boiling, chemical treatment, and filtering. If you boil water, it's recommended that you do so for ten to fifteen minutes. This is often impractical because you're forced to exhaust a great deal of your fuel supply. You can opt for chemical treatment, which will kill Giardia but will not take care of other chemical pollutants. Another drawback to chemical treatments is the unpleasant taste of the water after it's treated. You can remedy this by adding powdered drink mix to the water. Filters are the preferred method for treating water. Many filters remove Giardia, organic and inorganic contaminants, and don't leave an aftertaste. Water filters are far from perfect as they can easily become clogged or leak if a gasket wears out. It's always a good idea to carry a backup supply of chemical treatment tablets in case your filter decides to quit on you.

Food. If we're talking about survival, you can go days without food, as long as you have water. But we're also talking about comfort. Try to avoid foods that are high in sugar and fat like candy bars and potato chips. These food types are harder to digest and are low in nutritional value. Instead, bring along foods that are easy to pack, nutritious, and high in energy (e.g., bagels, nutrition bars, dehydrated fruit, gorp, and jerky). If you are on an overnight trip, easy-to-fix dinners include rice mixes with dehydrated potatoes, corn, pasta with cheese sauce, and soup mixes. For a tasty breakfast, you can fix hot oatmeal with brown sugar and reconstituted milk powder topped off with banana chips. If you like a hot drink in the morning, bring along herbal tea bags or hot chocolate. If you are a coffee junkie, you can purchase coffee that is packaged like tea bags. You can prepackage all of your meals in heavy-duty resealable plastic bags to keep food from spilling in your pack. These bags can be reused to pack out trash.

Shelter. The type of shelter you choose depends less on the conditions than on your tolerance for discomfort. Shelter comes in many forms—tent, tarp, lean-to, bivy sack, cabin, cave, etc. If you're camping in the desert, a bivy sack may suffice, but if you're above the treeline and a storm is approaching, a better choice is a three- or four-season tent. Tents are the logical and most popular choice for most backpackers as they're lightweight and packable—and you can rest assured that you always have shelter from the elements. Before you leave on your trip, anticipate what the weather and terrain will be like and plan for the type of shelter that will work best for your comfort level (see Equipment later in this section).

Finding a campsite. If there are established campsites, stick to those. If not, start looking for a campsite early—around 3:30 or 4:00 p.m. Stop at the first decent site you see. Depending on the area, it could be a long time before you find another suitable location. Pitch your camp in an area that's level. Make sure the area is at least 200 feet from fragile areas like lakeshores, meadows, and stream banks. And try to avoid areas thick in underbrush, as they can harbor insects and provide cover for approaching animals.

If you are camping in stormy, rainy weather, look for a rock outcrop or a shelter in the trees to keep the wind from blowing your tent all night. Be sure that you don't camp under trees with dead limbs that might break off on top of you. Also, try to find an area that has an absorbent surface, such as sandy soil or forest duff. This, in addition to camping on a surface with a slight angle, will provide better drainage. By all means, don't dig trenches to provide drainage around your tent—remember you're practicing zero-impact camping.

If you're in bear country, steer clear of creekbeds or animal paths. If you see any signs of a bear's presence (i.e., scat, footprints), relocate. You'll need to find a campsite near a tall tree where you can hang your food and other items that may attract bears such as deodorant, toothpaste, or soap. Carry a lightweight nylon rope with which to hang your food. As a rule, you should hang your food at least 20 feet from the ground and 5 feet away from the tree trunk. You can put food and other items in a waterproof stuff sack and tie one end of the rope to the stuff sack. To get the other end of the rope over the tree branch, tie a good size rock to it, and gently toss the rock over the tree branch. Pull the stuff sack up until it reaches the top of the branch and tie it off securely. Don't hang your food near your tent! If possible, hang your food at least 100 feet away from your campsite. Alternatives to hanging your food are bear-proof plastic tubes and metal bear boxes.

Lastly, think of comfort. Lie on the ground where you intend to sleep and see if it's a good fit. For morning warmth, have your tent face east.

First Aid

I know you're tough, but get 10 miles into the woods and develop a blister and you'll wish you had carried that first-aid kit. Many companies produce light-weight, compact kits. Just make sure yours contains at least the following:

- adhesive bandages
- moleskin or duct tape
- various sterile gauze and dressings
- white surgical tape
- an Ace bandage
- an antihistamine
- aspirin
- Betadine solution
- a first-aid book
- antacid tablets
- tweezers
- scissors
- antibacterial wipes
- triple-antibiotic ointment
- plastic gloves
- sterile cotton tip applicators
- syrup of ipecac (to induce vomiting)
- thermometer
- wire splint

Here are a few tips for dealing with and hopefully preventing certain ailments:

Sunburn. Take along sunscreen or sun block, protective clothing, and a wide-brimmed hat. If you do get a sunburn, treat the area with aloe vera gel, and protect the area from further sun exposure. At higher elevations, the sun's radiation can be particularly damaging to skin. Remember that your eyes are vulnerable to this radiation as well. Sunglasses can be a good way to prevent headaches and permanent eye damage from the sun, especially in places where light-colored rock or patches of snow reflect light up in your face.

Blisters. Be prepared to take care of these hike-spoilers by carrying moleskin (a lightly padded adhesive), gauze and tape, or adhesive bandages. An effective way to apply moleskin is to cut out a circle of moleskin and remove the center—like a doughnut—and place it over the blistered area. Cutting the center out will reduce the pressure applied to the sensitive skin. Other products can help you combat blisters. Some are applied to suspicious hot spots before a blister forms to help decrease friction to that area, while others are applied to the blister after it has popped to help prevent further irritation.

Insect bites and stings. You can treat most insect bites and stings by applying hydrocortisone 1% cream topically and taking a pain medication such as ibuprofen or acetaminophen to reduce swelling. If you forgot to pack these items, a cold compress or a paste of mud and ashes can sometimes assuage the itching and discomfort. Remove any stingers by using tweezers or scraping the area with your fingernail or a knife blade. Don't pinch the area as you'll only spread the venom.

Some hikers are highly sensitive to bites and stings and may have a serious allergic reaction that can be life threatening. Symptoms of a serious allergic reaction can include wheezing, an asthmatic attack, and shock. The treatment for this severe type of reaction is epinephrine. If you know that you are sensitive to bites and stings, carry a pre-packaged kit of epinephrine, which can be obtained only by prescription from your doctor.

Ticks. Ticks can carry diseases such as Rocky Mountain spotted fever and Lyme disease. The best defense is, of course, prevention. If you know you're going to be hiking through an area littered with ticks, wear long pants and a long sleeved shirt. You can apply a permethrin repellent to your clothing and a Deet repellent to exposed skin. At the end of your hike, do a spot check for ticks (and insects in general). If you do find a tick, grab the head of the tick firmly—with a pair of tweezers if you have them—and gently pull it away from the skin with a twisting motion. Sometimes the mouth parts linger, embedded in your skin. If this happens, try to remove them with a disinfected needle. Clean the affected area with an antibacterial cleanser and then apply triple antibiotic ointment. Monitor the area for a few days. If irritation persists or a white spot develops, see a doctor for possible infection.

Poison ivy, oak, and sumac. These skin irritants can be found most anywhere in North America and come in the form of a bush or a vine, having leaflets in groups of three, five, seven, or nine. Learn how to spot the plants. The oil they secrete can cause an allergic reaction in the form of blisters, usually about twelve hours after exposure. The itchy rash can last from ten days to several weeks. The best defense against these irritants is to wear clothing that covers the arms, legs and torso. For summer, zip-off cargo pants come in handy. There are also nonprescription lotions you can apply to exposed skin that guard against the effects of poison ivy/oak/sumac and can be washed off with soap and water. If you think you were in contact with the plants, after hiking (or even on the trail during longer hikes) wash with soap and water. Taking a hot shower with soap after you return home from your hike will also help to remove any lingering oil from your skin. Should you contract a rash from any of these plants, use an antihistamine to reduce the itching. If the rash is localized, create a light bleach/water wash to dry up the area. If the rash has spread, either tough it out or see your doctor about getting a dose of cortisone (available both orally and by injection).

Snakebites. Snakebites are rare in North America. Unless startled or provoked, most snakes will not bite. If you are wise to their habitats and keep a careful eye on the trail, you should be fine. When stepping over logs, first step on the log, making sure you can see what's on the other side before stepping down. Though your chances of being struck are slim, it's wise to know what to do if you are.

If a *nonpoisonous* snake bites you, allow the wound to bleed a small amount and then cleanse the wounded area with a Betadine solution (10% povidone iodine). Rinse the wound with clean water (preferably) or fresh urine (it might sound ugly, but it's sterile). Once the area is clean, cover it with triple antibiotic ointment and a clean bandage. Remember, most residual damage from snakebites, poisonous or otherwise, comes from infection, not the snake's venom. Keep the area as clean as possible and get medical attention immediately.

If somebody in your party is bitten by a poisonous snake, follow these steps:

1. Calm the patient.
2. Remove jewelry, watches, and restrictive clothing, and immobilize the affected limb. Do not elevate the injury. Medical opinions vary on whether the area should be lower or level with the heart, but the consensus is that it should not be above it.
3. Make a note of the circumference of the limb at the bite site and at various points above the site as well. This will help you monitor swelling.
4. Evacuate your victim. Ideally he should be carried out to minimize movement. If the victim appears to be doing okay, he can walk. Stop and rest frequently, and if the swelling appears to be spreading or the patient's symptoms increase, change your plan and find a way to get your patient transported.
5. If you are waiting for rescue, make sure to keep your patient comfortable and hydrated (unless he begins vomiting).

Snakebite treatment is rife with old-fashioned remedies: You used to be told to cut and suck the venom out of the bite site or to use a suction cup extractor for the same purpose; applying an electric shock to the area was even in vogue for a while. Do not do any of these things. Do not apply ice, do not give your patient painkillers, and do not apply a tourniquet. All you really want to do is keep your patient calm and get help. If you're alone and have to hike out, don't run—you'll only increase the flow of blood throughout your system. Instead, walk calmly.

Dehydration. Have you ever hiked in hot weather and had a roaring headache and felt fatigued after only a few miles? More than likely you were dehydrated. Symptoms of dehydration include fatigue, headache, and decreased coordination and judgment. When you are hiking, your body's rate of fluid loss depends on the outside temperature, humidity, altitude, and your activity level. On average, a hiker walking in warm weather will lose four liters of fluid a day. That fluid loss is easily replaced by normal consumption of liquids and food. However, if a hiker is walking briskly in hot, dry weather and hauling a heavy pack, he or she can lose one to three liters of water an hour. It's important to always carry plenty of water and to stop often and drink fluids regularly, even if you aren't thirsty.

Heat exhaustion is the result of a loss of large amounts of electrolytes and often occurs if a hiker is dehydrated and has been under heavy exertion. Common symptoms of heat exhaustion include cramping, exhaustion, fatigue, lightheadedness, and nausea. You can treat heat exhaustion by getting out of the sun and drinking an electrolyte solution made up of one teaspoon of salt and one tablespoon of sugar dissolved in a liter of water. Drink this solution slowly over a period of one hour. Drinking plenty of fluids (preferably an electrolyte solution/sports drink) can prevent heat exhaustion. Avoid hiking during the hottest parts of the day, and wear breathable clothing, a wide-brimmed hat, and sunglasses.

Hypothermia is one of the biggest dangers in the backcountry, especially for day hikers in the summertime. That may sound strange, but imagine starting out on a hike in midsummer when it's sunny and 80 degrees out. You're clad in nylon shorts and a cotton T-shirt. About halfway through your hike, the sky begins to cloud up, and in the next hour a light drizzle begins to fall and the wind starts to pick up. Before you know it, you are soaking wet and shivering—the perfect recipe for hypothermia. More advanced signs include decreased coordination, slurred speech, and blurred vision. When a victim's temperature falls below 92 degrees, the blood pressure and pulse plummet, possibly leading to coma and death.

To avoid hypothermia, always bring a windproof/rainproof shell, a fleece jacket, long underwear made of a breathable, synthetic fiber, gloves, and hat when you are hiking in the mountains. Learn to adjust your clothing layers based on the temperature. If you are climbing uphill at a moderate pace you will stay warm, but when you stop for a break you'll become cold quickly, unless you add more layers of clothing.

If a hiker is showing advanced signs of hypothermia, dress him or her in dry clothes and make sure he or she is wearing a hat and gloves. Place the person in a sleeping bag in a tent or shelter that will protect him or her from the wind and other elements. Give the person warm fluids to drink and keep him awake.

Frostbite. When the mercury dips below 32 degrees, your extremities begin to chill. If a persistent chill attacks a localized area, say, your hands or your toes, the circulatory system reacts by cutting off blood flow to the affected area—the idea being to protect and preserve the body's overall temperature. And so it's death by attrition for the affected area. Ice crystals start to form from the water in the cells of the neglected tissue. Deprived of heat, nourishment, and now water, the tissue literally starves. This is frostbite.

Prevention is your best defense against this situation. Most prone to frostbite are your face, hands, and feet, so protect these areas well. Wool is the traditional material of choice because it provides ample air space for insulation and draws moisture away from the skin. Synthetic fabrics, however, have made great strides in the cold weather clothing market. Do your research. A pair of light silk liners under your regular gloves is a good trick for keeping warm. They afford some additional warmth, but more importantly they'll allow you to remove your mitts for tedious work without exposing the skin.

If your feet or hands start to feel cold or numb due to the elements, warm them as quickly as possible. Place cold hands under your armpits or bury them in your crotch. If your feet are cold, change your socks. If there's plenty of room in your boots, add another pair of socks. Do remember, though, that constricting your feet in tight boots can restrict blood flow and actually make your feet colder more quickly. Your socks need to have breathing room if they're going to be effective. Dead air provides insulation. If your face is cold, place your warm hands over your face, or simply wear a head stocking.

Should your skin go numb and start to appear white and waxy, chances are you've got or are developing frostbite. Don't try to thaw the area unless you can maintain the warmth. In other words, don't stop to warm up your frostbitten feet only to head back on the trail. You'll do more damage than good. Tests have shown that hikers who walked on thawed feet did more harm, and endured more pain, than hikers who left the affected areas alone. Do your best to get out of the cold entirely and seek medical attention—which usually consists of performing a rapid rewarming in water for twenty to thirty minutes.

The overall objective in preventing both hypothermia and frostbite is to keep the body's core warm. Protect key areas where heat escapes, like the top of the head, and maintain the proper nutrition level. Foods that are high in calories aid the body in producing heat. Never smoke or drink when you're in situations where the cold is threatening. By affecting blood flow, these activities ultimately cool the body's core temperature.

Altitude sickness (AMS). High lofty peaks, clear alpine lakes, and vast mountain views beckon hikers to the high country. But those who like to venture high may become victims of altitude sickness (also known as Acute Mountain Sickness—AMS). Altitude sickness is your body's reaction to insufficient oxygen in the blood due to decreased barometric pressure. While some hikers may feel light-headed, nauseous, and experience shortness of breath at 7,000 feet, others may not experience these symptoms until they reach 10,000 feet or higher.

Slowing your ascent to high places and giving your body a chance to acclimatize to the higher elevations can prevent altitude sickness. For example, if you live at sea level and are planning a weeklong backpacking trip to elevations between

7,000 and 12,000 feet, start by staying below 7,000 feet for one night, then move to between 7,000 and 10,000 feet for another night or two. Avoid strenuous exertion and alcohol to give your body a chance to adjust to the new altitude. It's also important to eat light food and drink plenty of nonalcoholic fluids, preferably water. Loss of appetite at altitude is common, but you must eat!

Most hikers who experience mild to moderate AMS develop a headache and/ or nausea, grow lethargic, and have problems sleeping. The treatment for AMS is simple: stop heading uphill. Keep eating and drinking water and take meds for the headache. You actually need to take more breaths at altitude than at sea level, so breathe a little faster without hyperventilating. If symptoms don't improve over twenty-four to forty-eight hours, descend. Once a victim descends about 2,000 to 3,000 feet, his signs will usually begin to diminish.

Severe AMS comes in two forms: High Altitude Pulmonary Edema (HAPE) and High Altitude Cerebral Edema (HACE). HAPE, an accumulation of fluid in the lungs, can occur above 8,000 feet. Symptoms include rapid heart rate, shortness of breath at rest, AMS symptoms, dry cough developing into a wet cough, gurgling sounds, flu-like or bronchitis symptoms, and lack of muscle coordination. HAPE is life threatening so descend immediately, at least 2,000 to 4,000 feet. HACE usually occurs above 12,000 feet but sometimes occurs above 10,000 feet. Symptoms are similar to HAPE but also include seizures, hallucinations, paralysis, and vision disturbances. Descend immediately—HACE is also life threatening.

Hantavirus Pulmonary Syndrome (HPS). Deer mice spread the virus that causes HPS, and humans contract it from breathing it in, usually when they've disturbed an area with dust and mice feces from nests or surfaces with mice droppings or urine. Exposure to large numbers of rodents and their feces or urine presents the greatest risk. As hikers, we sometimes enter old buildings, and often deer mice live in these places. We may not be around long enough to be exposed, but do be aware of this disease. About half the people who develop HPS die. Symptoms are flu-like and appear about two to three weeks after exposure. After initial symptoms, a dry cough and shortness of breath follow. Breathing is difficult. If you even think you might have HPS, see a doctor immediately!

Natural Hazards

Besides tripping over a rock or tree root on the trail, there are some real hazards to be aware of while hiking. Even if where you're hiking doesn't have the plethora of poisonous snakes and plants, insects, and grizzly bears found in other parts of the United States, there are a few weather conditions and predators you may need to take into account.

Lightning. Thunderstorms build over the mountains almost every day during the summer. Lightning is generated by thunderheads and can strike without warning, even several miles away from the nearest overhead cloud. The best rule of thumb is to start leaving exposed peaks, ridges, and canyon rims by about noon. This time can vary a little depending on storm buildup. Keep an eye on cloud formation and don't underestimate how fast a storm can build. The bigger they get, the more likely a thunderstorm will happen. Lightning takes the path of least resistance, so if you're the high point, it might choose you. Ducking under a rock overhang is dangerous as you form the shortest path between the rock and ground. If you dash below treeline, avoid standing under the only or the tallest tree. If you are caught above treeline, stay away from anything metal you might be carrying, Move down off the ridge slightly to a low, treeless point and squat until the storm passes. If you have an insulating pad, squat on it. Avoid having both your hands and feet touching the ground at once and never lay flat. If you hear a buzzing sound or feel your hair standing on end, move quickly as an electrical charge is building up.

Flash floods. On July 31, 1976, a torrential downpour unleashed by a thunderstorm dumped tons of water into the Big Thompson watershed near Estes Park. Within hours, a wall of water moved down the narrow canyon killing 139 people and causing more than $30 million in property damage. The spooky thing about flash floods, especially in western canyons, is that they can appear out of nowhere from a storm many miles away. While hiking or driving in canyons, keep an eye on the weather. Always climb to safety if danger threatens. Flash floods usually subside quickly, so be patient and don't cross a swollen stream.

Bears. Most of the United States (outside of the Pacific Northwest and parts of the Northern Rockies) does not have a grizzly bear population, although some rumors exist about sightings where there should be none. Black bears are plentiful, however. Here are some tips in case you and a bear scare each other. Most of all, avoid surprising a bear. Talk or sing where visibility or hearing are limited, such as along a rushing creek or in thick brush. In grizzly country especially, carry bear spray in a holster on your pack belt where you can quickly grab it. While hiking, watch for bear tracks (five toes), droppings (sizable with leaves, partly digested berries, seeds, and/or animal fur), or rocks and roots along the trail that show signs of being dug up (this could be a bear looking for bugs to eat). Keep a clean camp, hang food or use bearproof storage containers, and don't sleep in the clothes you wore while cooking. Be especially careful to avoid getting between a mother and her cubs. In late summer and fall bears are busy eating to fatten up for winter, so be extra careful around berry bushes and oakbrush. If you do encounter a bear, move away slowly while facing the bear, talk softly, and avoid direct eye contact. Give the bear room to escape. Since bears are very curious, it might stand upright to get a better whiff of you, and it may even charge you to try to intimidate you. Try to stay calm. If a black bear attacks you, fight back with anything you have handy. If a grizzly bear attacks you, your best option is to "play dead" by lying face down on the ground and covering the back of your neck and head with your hands. Unleashed dogs have been known to come running back to their owners with a bear close behind. Keep your dog on a leash or leave it at home.

Mountain lions. Mountain lions appear to be getting more comfortable around humans as long as deer (their favorite prey) are in an area with adequate cover. Usually elusive and quiet, lions rarely attack people. If you meet a lion, give it a chance to escape. Stay calm and talk firmly to it. Back away slowly while facing the lion. If you run, you'll only encourage the cat to chase you. Make yourself look large by opening a jacket, if you have one, or waving your hiking poles. If the lion behaves aggressively throw stones, sticks, or whatever you can while remaining tall. If a lion does attack, fight for your life with anything you can grab.

Other considerations. Hunting is a popular sport in the United States, especially during rifle season in October and November. Hiking is still enjoyable in those months in many areas, so just take a few precautions. First, learn when the different hunting seasons start and end in the area in which you'll be hiking. During this time frame, be sure to wear at least a blaze orange hat, and possibly put an orange vest over your pack. Don't be surprised to see hunters in camo outfits carrying bows or rifles around during their season. If you would feel more comfortable without hunters around, hike in national parks and monuments or state and local parks where hunting is not allowed.

Navigation

Whether you are going on a short hike in a familiar area or planning a week-long backpack trip, you should always be equipped with the proper navigational equipment—at the very least a detailed map and a sturdy compass.

Maps. There are many different types of maps available to help you find your way on the trail. Easiest to find are Forest Service maps and BLM (Bureau of Land Management) maps. These maps tend to cover large areas, so be sure they are detailed enough for your particular trip. You can also obtain National Park maps as well as high quality maps from private companies and trail groups. These maps can be obtained either from outdoor stores or ranger stations.

U.S. Geological Survey topographic maps are particularly popular with hikers—especially serious backcountry hikers. These maps contain the standard map symbols such as roads, lakes, and rivers, as well as contour lines that show the details of the trail terrain like ridges, valleys, passes, and mountain peaks. The 7.5-minute series (1 inch on the map equals approximately 2/5 mile on the ground) provides the closest inspection available. USGS maps are available by mail (U.S. Geological Survey, Map Distribution Branch, P.O. Box 25286, Denver, CO 80225), or at mapping.usgs.gov/esic/to_order.html.

If you want to check out the high-tech world of maps, you can purchase topographic maps on CD-ROM. These software-mapping programs let you select a route on your computer, print it out, then take it with you on the trail. Some software mapping programs let you insert symbols and labels, download waypoints from a GPS unit, and export the maps to other software programs.

The art of map reading is a skill that you can develop by first practicing in an area you are familiar with. To begin, orient the map so the map is lined up in the correct direction (i.e. north on the map is lined up with true north). Next, familiarize yourself with the map symbols and try and match them up with terrain features around you such as a high ridge, mountain peak, river, or lake. If you are practicing with a USGS map, notice the contour lines. On gentler terrain these contour lines are spaced farther apart, and on steeper terrain they are closer together. Pick a short loop trail, and stop frequently to check your position on the map. As you practice map reading, you'll learn how to anticipate a steep section on the trail or a good place to take a rest break, and so on.

Compasses. First off, the sun is not a substitute for a compass. So, what kind of compass should you have? Here are some characteristics you should look for: a rectangular base with detailed scales, a liquid-filled housing, protective housing, a sighting line on the mirror, luminous alignment and back-bearing arrows, a luminous north-seeking arrow, and a well-defined bezel ring.

You can learn compass basics by reading the detailed instructions included with your compass. If you want to fine-tune your compass skills, sign up for an orienteering class or purchase a book on compass reading. Once you've learned the basic skills of using a compass, remember to practice these skills before you head into the backcountry.

If you are a klutz at using a compass, you may be interested in checking out the technical wizardry of the GPS (Global Positioning System) device. The GPS was developed by the Pentagon and works off twenty-four NAVSTAR satellites, which were designed to guide missiles to their targets. A GPS device is a handheld unit that calculates your latitude and longitude with the easy press of a button. The Department of Defense used to scramble the satellite signals a bit to prevent civilians (and spies!) from getting extremely accurate readings, but that practice was discontinued in May 2000, and GPS units now provide nearly pinpoint accuracy (within 30 to 60 feet).

There are many different types of GPS units available and they range in price from $100 to $400. In general, all GPS units have a display screen and keypad where you input information. In addition to acting as a compass, the unit allows you to plot your route, easily retrace your path, track your travelling speed, find the mileage between waypoints, and calculate the total mileage of your route.

Before you purchase a GPS unit, keep in mind that these devices don't pick up signals indoors, in heavily wooded areas, on mountain peaks, or in deep valleys. Also, batteries can wear out or other technical problems can develop. A GPS unit should be used in conjunction with a map and compass, not in place of those items.

Pedometers. A pedometer is a small, clip-on unit with a digital display that calculates your hiking distance in miles or kilometers based on your walking stride. Some units also calculate the calories you burn and your total hiking time. Pedometers are available at most large outdoor stores and range in price from $20 to $40.

Trip Planning

Planning your hiking adventure begins with letting a friend or relative know your trip itinerary so they can call for help if you don't return at your scheduled time. Your next task is to make sure you are outfitted to experience the risks and rewards of the trail. This section highlights gear and clothing you may want to take with you to get the most out of your hike.

Day Hikes

- whistle
- camera
- compass/GPS unit
- pedometer
- daypack
- first-aid kit
- food
- guidebook
- headlamp/flashlight with extra batteries and bulbs
- hat
- insect repellent
- knife/multipurpose tool
- map
- matches in waterproof container and fire starter
- fleece jacket
- rain gear
- space blanket
- sunglasses
- sunscreen
- swimsuit and/or fishing gear (if hiking to a lake)
- watch
- water
- water bottles/water hydration system

Overnight Trip

- backpack and waterproof rain cover
- backpacker's trowel
- bandanna

- biodegradable soap
- pot scrubber
- collapsible water container (2–3 gallon capacity)
- clothing—extra wool socks, shirt and shorts
- cook set/utensils
- ditty bags to store gear
- extra plastic resealable bags
- gaiters
- garbage bag
- ground cloth
- journal/pen
- nylon rope to hang food
- long underwear
- permit (if required)
- rain jacket and pants
- sandals to wear around camp and to ford streams
- sleeping bag
- waterproof stuff sack
- sleeping pad
- small bath towel
- stove and fuel
- tent
- toiletry items
- water filter
- whistle

Equipment

With the outdoor market currently flooded with products, many of which are pure gimmickry, it seems impossible to both differentiate and choose. Do I really need a tropical-fish-lined collapsible shower? (No, you don't.) The only defense against the maddening quantity of items thrust in your face is to think practically—and to do so before you go shopping. The worst buys are impulsive buys. Since most name brands will differ only slightly in quality, it's best to know what you're looking for in terms of function. Buy only what you need. You will, don't forget, be carrying what you've bought on your back. Here are some things to keep in mind before you go shopping.

Clothes. Clothing is your against Mother Nature's little surprises. Hikers should be prepared for any possibility, especially when hiking in mountainous areas. Adequate rain protection and extra layers of clothing are a good idea. In summer, a wide-brimmed hat can help keep the sun at bay. In the winter months the first layer you'll want to wear is a "wicking" layer of long underwear that keeps perspiration away from your skin. Wear long underwear made from synthetic fibers that wick moisture away from the skin and draw it toward the next layer of clothing, where it then evaporates. Avoid wearing long underwear made of cotton as it is slow to dry and keeps moisture next to your skin.

The second layer you'll wear is the "insulating" layer. Aside from keeping you warm, this layer needs to "breathe" so you stay dry while hiking. A fabric that provides insulation and dries quickly is fleece. It's interesting to note that this one-of-a-kind fabric is made out of recycled plastic. Purchasing a zip-up jacket made of this material is highly recommended.

The last line of layering defense is the "shell" layer. You'll need some type of waterproof, windproof, breathable jacket that will fit over all of your other layers. It should have a large hood that fits over a hat. You'll also need a good pair of rain pants made from a similar waterproof, breathable fabric. Some Gore-Tex jackets cost as much as $500, but you should know that there are more affordable fabrics out there that work just as well.

Now that you've learned the basics of layering, you can't forget to protect your hands and face. In cold, windy, or rainy weather you'll need a hat made of wool or fleece and insulated, waterproof gloves that will keep your hands warm and toasty. As mentioned earlier, buying an additional pair of light silk liners to wear under your regular gloves is a good idea.

Footwear. If you have any extra money to spend on your trip, put that money into boots or trail shoes. Poor shoes will bring a hike to a halt faster than anything else. To avoid this annoyance, buy shoes that provide support and are lightweight and flexible. A lightweight hiking boot is better than a heavy, leather mountaineering boot for most day hikes and backpacking. Trail running shoes provide a little extra cushion and are made in a high-top style that many people wear for hiking. These running shoes are lighter, more flexible, and more breathable than hiking boots. If you know you'll be hiking in wet weather often, purchase boots or shoes with a Gore-Tex liner, which will help keep your feet dry.

When buying your boots, be sure to wear the same type of socks you'll be wearing on the trail. If the boots you're buying are for cold weather hiking, try the boots on while wearing two pairs of socks. Speaking of socks, a good cold weather sock combination is to wear a thinner sock made of wool or polypropylene covered by a heavier outer sock made of wool or a synthetic/wool mix. The inner sock protects the foot from the rubbing effects of the outer sock and prevents blisters. Many outdoor stores have some type of ramp to simulate hiking uphill and downhill. Be sure to take advantage of this test, as toe-jamming boot fronts can be very painful and debilitating on the downhill trek.

Once you've purchased your footwear, be sure to break them in before you hit the trail. New footwear is often stiff and needs to be stretched and molded to your foot.

Hiking poles. Hiking poles help with balance, and more importantly take pressure off your knees. The ones with shock absorbers are easier on your elbows and knees. Some poles even come with a camera attachment to be used as a monopod. And heaven forbid you meet a mountain lion, bear, or unfriendly dog, the poles can make you look a lot bigger.

Backpacks. No matter what type of hiking you do you'll need a pack of some sort to carry the basic trail essentials. There are a variety of backpacks on the market, but let's first discuss what you intend to use it for. Day hikes or overnight trips?

If you plan on doing a day hike, a daypack should have some of the following characteristics: a padded hip belt that's at least 2 inches in diameter (avoid packs with only a small nylon piece of webbing for a hip belt); a chest strap (the chest strap helps stabilize the pack against your body); external pockets to carry water and other items that you want easy access to; an internal pocket to hold keys, a knife, a wallet, and other miscellaneous items; an external lashing system to hold a jacket; and, if you so desire, a hydration pocket for carrying a hydration system (which consists of a water bladder with an attachable drinking hose).

For short hikes, some hikers like to use a fanny pack to store just a camera, food, a compass, a map, and other trail essentials. Most fanny packs have pockets for two water bottles and a padded hip belt.

If you intend to do an extended, overnight trip, there are multiple considerations. First off, you need to decide what kind of framed pack you want. There are two backpack types for backpacking: the internal frame and the external frame. An internal frame pack rests closer to your body, making it more stable and easier to balance when hiking over rough terrain. An external frame pack is just that, an aluminum frame attached to the exterior of the pack. Some hikers consider an external frame pack to be better for long backpack trips because it distributes the pack weight better and allows you to carry heavier loads. It's often easier to pack, and your gear is more accessible. It also offers better back ventilation in hot weather.

The most critical measurement for fitting a pack is torso length. The pack needs to rest evenly on your hips without sagging. A good pack will come in two or three sizes and have straps and hip belts that are adjustable according to your body size and characteristics.

When you purchase a backpack, go to an outdoor store with salespeople who are knowledgeable in how to properly fit a pack. Once the pack is fitted for you, load the pack with the amount of weight you plan on taking on the trail. The weight of the pack should be distributed evenly and you should be able to swing your arms and walk briskly without feeling out of balance. Another good technique for evaluating a pack is to walk up and down stairs and make quick turns to the right and to the left to be sure the pack doesn't feel out of balance. Other features that are nice to have on a backpack include a removable day pack or fanny pack, external pockets for extra water, and extra lash points to attach a jacket or other items.

Sleeping bags and pads. Sleeping bags are rated by temperature. You can purchase a bag made with synthetic insulation, or you can buy a goose down bag. Goose down bags are more expensive, but they have a higher insulating capacity by weight and will keep their loft longer. You'll want to purchase a bag with a temperature rating that fits the time of year and conditions you are most likely to camp in. One caveat: The techno-standard for temperature ratings is far from perfect. Ratings vary from manufacturer to manufacturer, so to protect yourself you should purchase a bag rated 10 to 15 degrees below the temperature you expect to be camping in. Synthetic bags are more resistant to water than down bags, but many down bags are now made with a Gore-Tex shell that helps to repel water. Down bags are also more compressible than synthetic bags and take up less room in your pack, which is an important consideration if you are planning a multiday backpack trip. Features to look for in a sleeping bag include a mummy style bag, a hood you can cinch down around your head in cold weather, and draft tubes along the zippers that help keep heat in and drafts out.

You'll also want a sleeping pad to provide insulation and padding from the cold ground. There are different types of sleeping pads available, from the more expensive self-inflating air mattresses to the less expensive closed-cell foam pads. Self-inflating air mattresses are usually heavier than closed-cell foam mattresses and are prone to punctures.

Tents. The tent is your home away from home while on the trail. It provides protection from wind, rain, snow, and insects. A three-season tent is a good choice for backpacking and can range in price from $100 to $500. These lightweight and versatile tents provide protection in all types of weather, except heavy snowstorms or high winds, and range in weight from four to eight pounds. Look for a tent that's easy to set up and will easily fit two people with gear. Dome type tents usually offer more headroom and places to store gear. Other handy tent features include a vestibule where you can store wet boots and backpacks. Some nice-to-have items in a tent include interior pockets to store small items and lashing points to hang a clothesline. Most three-season tents also come with stakes so you can secure the tent in high winds. Before you purchase a tent, set it up and take it down a few times to be sure it is easy to handle. Also, sit inside the tent and make sure it has enough room for you and your gear.

Cell phones. Many hikers carry their cell phones into the backcountry in case of emergency. That's fine, but please know that cell phone coverage is often poor to nonexistent in valleys, canyons, and thick forest. More importantly people have started to call for help because they're tired or lost. Let's go back to being prepared. You are responsible for yourself in the backcountry. Use your brain to avoid problems, and if you do encounter one, first use your brain to try to correct the situation. Only use your cell phone, if it works, in true emergencies. If it doesn't work down low in a valley, try hiking to a high point where you might get reception.

Hiking with Children

Hiking with children isn't a matter of how many miles you can cover or how much elevation gain you make in a day; it's about seeing and experiencing nature through their eyes.

Kids like to explore and have fun. They like to stop and point out bugs and plants, look under rocks, jump in puddles, and throw sticks. If you're taking a toddler or young child on a hike, start with a trail that you're familiar with. Trails that have interesting things for kids, like piles of leaves to play in or a small stream to wade through during the summer, will make the hike much more enjoyable for them and will keep them from getting bored.

You can keep your child's attention if you have a strategy before starting on the trail. Using games is not only an effective way to keep a child's attention, it's also a great way to teach him or her about nature. Quiz children on the names of plants and animals. Pick up a family-friendly outdoor hobby like Geocaching (www.geocaching.com) or Letterboxing (www.atlasquest.com), both of which combine the outdoors, clue-solving, and treasure hunting. If your children are old enough, let them carry their own daypack filled with snacks and water. So that you are sure to go at their pace and not yours, let them lead the way. Playing follow the leader works particularly well when you have a group of children. Have each child take a turn at being the leader.

With children, a lot of clothing is key. The only thing predictable about weather is that it will change. Especially in mountainous areas, weather can change dramatically in a very short time. Always bring extra clothing for children, regardless of the season. In the winter, have your children wear wool socks, and warm layers such as long underwear, a fleece jacket and hat, wool mittens, and good rain gear. It's not a bad idea to have these along in late fall and early spring as well. Good footwear is also important. A sturdy pair of high top tennis shoes or lightweight hiking boots are the best bet for little ones. If you're hiking in the summer near a lake or stream, bring along a pair of old sneakers that your child can put on when he wants to go exploring in the water. Remember when you're near any type of water, always watch your child at all times. Also, keep a close eye on teething toddlers who may decide a rock or leaf of poison oak is an interesting item to put in their mouth.

From spring through fall, you'll want your kids to wear a wide-brimmed hat to keep their face, head, and ears protected from the hot sun. Also, make sure your children wear sunscreen at all times. Choose a brand without Paba—children have sensitive skin and may have an allergic reaction to sunscreen that contains Paba. If you are hiking with a child younger than six months, don't use sunscreen or insect repellent. Instead, be sure that their head, face, neck, and ears are protected from the sun with a wide-brimmed hat, and that all other skin exposed to the sun is protected with the appropriate clothing.

Remember that food is fun. Kids like snacks so it's important to bring a lot of munchies for the trail. Stopping often for snack breaks is a fun way to keep the trail interesting. Raisins, apples, granola bars, crackers and cheese, cereal, and trail mix all make great snacks. Also, a few of their favorite candy treats can go a long way toward heading off a fit of fussing. If your child is old enough to carry her own backpack, let him or her fill it with some lightweight "comfort" items such as a doll, a small stuffed animal, or a little toy (you'll have to draw the line at bringing the ten-pound Tonka truck). If your kids don't like drinking water, you can bring some powdered drink mix or a juice box.

Avoid poorly designed child-carrying packs—you don't want to break your back carrying your child. Most child-carrying backpacks designed to hold a forty-pound child will contain a large carrying pocket to hold diapers and other items. Some have an optional rain/sun hood.

Hiking with Your Dog

Bringing your furry friend with you is always more fun than leaving him behind. Our canine pals make great trail buddies because they never complain and always make good company. Hiking with your dog can be a rewarding experience, especially if you plan ahead.

Getting your dog in shape. Before you plan outdoor adventures with your dog, make sure he's in shape for the trail. Getting your dog into shape takes the same discipline as getting yourself into shape, but luckily, your dog can get in shape with you. Take your dog with you on your daily runs or walks. If there is a park near your house, hit a tennis ball or play Frisbee with your dog.

Swimming is also a great way to get your dog into shape. If there is a lake or river near where you live and your dog likes water, have him retrieve a ball or stick. Gradually build your dog's stamina up over a two- to three-month period. A good rule of thumb is to assume that your dog will travel twice as far as you on the trail. If you plan on doing a 5-mile hike, be sure your dog is in shape for a 10-mile hike.

Training your dog for the trail. Before you go on your first hiking adventure with your dog, be sure he has a firm grasp on the basics of canine etiquette and behavior. Make sure he can sit, lie down, stay, and come. One of the most important commands you can teach your canine pal is to "come" under any situation. It's easy for your friend's nose to lead him astray or possibly get lost. Another helpful command is the "get behind" command. When you're on a hiking trail that's narrow, you can have your dog follow behind you when other trail users approach. Nothing is more bothersome than an enthusiastic dog that runs back and forth on the trail and disrupts the peace of the trail for others—or, worse, jumps up on other hikers and gets them muddy. When you see other trail users approaching you on the trail, give them the right of way by quietly stepping off the trail and making your dog lie down and stay until they pass.

Equipment. The most critical pieces of equipment you can invest in for your dog are proper identification and a sturdy leash. Flexi-leads work well for hiking because they give your dog more freedom to explore but still leave you in control. Make sure your dog has identification that includes your name and address and a number for your veterinarian. Other forms of identification for your dog include a tattoo or a microchip. You should consult your veterinarian for more information on these last two options.

The next piece of equipment you'll want to consider is a pack for your dog. By no means should you hold all of your dog's essentials in your pack—let him carry his own gear! Dogs that are in good shape can carry 30 to 40 percent of their own weight.

Most packs are fitted by a dog's weight and girth measurement. Companies that make dog packs generally include guidelines to help you pick out the size that's right for your dog. Some characteristics to look for when purchasing a pack for your dog include a harness that contains two padded girth straps, a padded chest strap, leash attachments, removable saddle bags, internal water bladders, and external gear cords.

You can introduce your dog to the pack by first placing the empty pack on his back and letting him wear it around the yard. Keep an eye on him during this first introduction. He may decide to chew through the straps if you aren't watching him closely. Once he learns to treat the pack as an object of fun and not a foreign enemy, fill the pack evenly on both sides with a few ounces of dog food in resealable plastic bags. Have your dog wear his pack on your daily walks for a period of two to three weeks. Each week add a little more weight to the pack until your dog will accept carrying the maximum amount of weight he can carry.

You can also purchase collapsible water and dog food bowls for your dog. These bowls are lightweight and can easily be stashed into your pack or your dog's. If you are hiking on rocky terrain or in the snow, you can purchase footwear for your dog that will protect his feet from cuts and bruises.

Always carry plastic bags to remove feces from the trail. It is a courtesy to other trail users and helps protect local wildlife.

The following is a list of items to bring when you take your dog hiking: collapsible water bowls, a comb, a collar and a leash, dog food, plastic bags for feces, a dog pack, flea/tick powder, paw protection, water, and a first-aid kit that contains eye ointment, tweezers, scissors, stretchy foot wrap, gauze, antibacterial wash, sterile cotton tip applicators, antibiotic ointment, and cotton wrap.

First aid for your dog. Your dog is just as prone—if not more prone—to getting in trouble on the trail as you are, so be prepared. Here's a rundown of the more likely misfortunes that might befall your little friend.

Bees and wasps. If a bee or wasp stings your dog, remove the stinger with a pair of tweezers and place a mudpack or a cloth dipped in cold water over the affected area.

Porcupines. One good reason to keep your dog on a leash is to prevent it from getting a nose full of porcupine quills. You may be able to remove the quills with pliers, but a veterinarian is the best person to do this nasty job because most dogs need to be sedated.

Heat stroke. Avoid hiking with your dog in really hot weather. Dogs with heat stroke will pant excessively, lie down and refuse to get up, and become lethargic and disoriented. If your dog shows any of these signs on the trail, have him lie down in the shade. If you are near a stream, pour cool water over your dog's entire body to help bring his body temperature back to normal.

Heartworm. Dogs get heartworms from mosquitoes which carry the disease in the prime mosquito months of July and August. Giving your dog a monthly pill prescribed by your veterinarian easily prevents this condition.

Plant pitfalls. One of the biggest plant hazards for dogs on the trail are foxtails. Foxtails are pointed grass seed heads that bury themselves in your friend's fur, between his toes, and even get in his ear canal. If left unattended, these nasty seeds can work their way under the skin and cause abscesses and other problems. If you have a long-haired dog, consider trimming the hair between his toes and giving him a summer haircut to help prevent foxtails from attaching to his fur. After every hike, always look over your dog for these seeds—especially between his toes and his ears.

Other plant hazards include burrs, thorns, thistles, and poison oak. If you find any burrs or thistles on your dog, remove them as soon as possible before they become an unmanageable mat. Thorns can pierce a dog's foot and cause a great deal of pain. If you see that your dog is lame, stop and check his feet for thorns. Dogs are immune to poison oak but they can pick up the sticky, oily substance from the plant and transfer it to you.

Protect those paws. Be sure to keep your dog's nails trimmed so he avoids getting soft tissue or joint injuries. If your dog slows and refuses to go on, check to see that his paws aren't torn or worn. You can protect your dog's paws from trail hazards such as sharp gravel, foxtails, lava scree, and thorns by purchasing dog boots.

Sunburn. If your dog has light skin he is an easy target for sunburn on his nose and other exposed skin areas. You can apply a nontoxic sunscreen to exposed skin areas that will help protect him from overexposure to the sun.

Ticks and fleas. Ticks can easily give your dog Lyme disease, as well as other diseases. Before you hit the trail, treat your dog with a flea and tick spray or powder.

You can also ask your veterinarian about a once-a-month pour-on treatment that repels fleas and ticks.

Mosquitoes and deer flies. These little flying machines can do a job on your dog's snout and ears. Best bet is to spray your dog with fly repellent for horses to discourage both pests.

Giardia. Dogs can get giardia, which results in diarrhea. It is usually not debilitating, but it's definitely messy. A vaccine against giardia is available.

Mushrooms. Make sure your dog doesn't sample mushrooms along the trail. They could be poisonous to him, but he doesn't know that.

When you are finally ready to hit the trail with your dog, keep in mind that national parks and many wilderness areas do not allow dogs on trails. Your best bet is to hike in national forests, BLM lands, and state parks. Always call ahead to see what the restrictions are.

Hike Index

About the Authors

Alexander Sakaru Goya is a lifelong backpacker, rock climber, and adventurer who has been sharing his outdoor experiences with the public since he was in elementary school, as a regular on the "Family Adventures" segments of the PBS television show *Outdoor Nevada*. As a teen he hiked Nevada's remote Ruby Crest Trail; the Grand Canyon rim to rim; from Juneau, Alaska, to Atlan, Canada; through numerous back trails of Hawaii; and throughout the rugged terrain of Zion National Park. He is coauthor of *Best Easy Day Hikes Cedar Rapids* and in his spare time is studying physics at the University of Nevada Las Vegas.

Lynn Goya grew up wandering the backwoods and open fields of Iowa. As an adult, she moved from coast to coast, and as a travel writer she has taken her family on a mission of discovery to find the little-known places and people that make each area unique. From hot spring waterfalls in Nevada to pink dolphins in the Amazon, she has shared her findings through her Emmy-nominated work on the PBS television show *Outdoor Nevada* and her national print work for *USA Today*, *Audubon* magazine, *Outside Family*, and others. Lynn is the author of *Fun with the Family in Las Vegas*, fourth edition, and coauthor of *Best Easy Day Hikes Cedar Rapids*.

Alexander and Lynn live in Boulder City, Nevada, the heart of the Mojave Desert, with Alan ("Dad"), Seiji, Chloe, and their mutt, Chase. Alexander and Lynn can be contacted at www.lynngoya.com.

Your next adventure begins here.

falcon.com

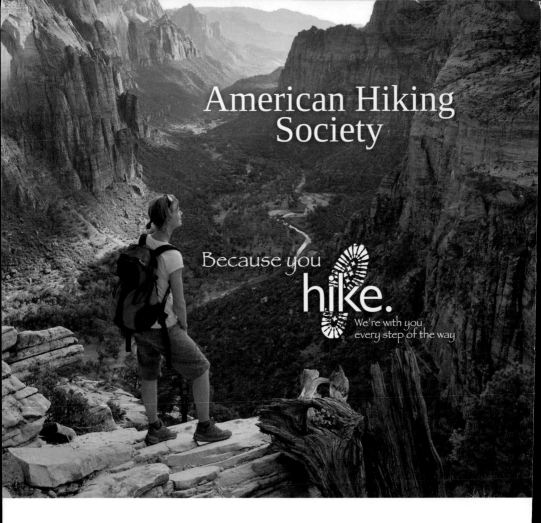

American Hiking Society

Because you **hike.**

We're with you every step of the way

As a national voice for hikers, **American Hiking Society** works every day:

- Building and maintaining hiking trails
- Educating and supporting hikers by providing information and resources
- Supporting hiking and trail organizations nationwide
- Speaking for hikers in the halls of Congress and with federal land managers

Whether you're a casual hiker or a seasoned backpacker, become a member of American Hiking Society and join the national hiking community! You'll enjoy great member benefits and help preserve the nation's hiking trails, so tomorrow's hike is even better than today's. We invite you to join us now!

American Hiking Society